Strengthened by the Gospel

New Testament Theology

Edited by Thomas R. Schreiner and Brian S. Rosner

The Beginning of the Gospel: A Theology of Mark, Peter Orr

From the Manger to the Throne: A Theology of Luke, Benjamin L. Gladd

The Mission of the Triune God: A Theology of Acts, Patrick Schreiner

Strengthened by the Gospel: A Theology of Romans, Brian S. Rosner

Ministry in the New Realm: A Theology of 2 Corinthians, Dane C. Ortlund

Christ Crucified: A Theology of Galatians, Thomas R. Schreiner

United to Christ, Walking in the Spirit: A Theology of Ephesians, Benjamin L. Merkle

Sharing Christ in Joy and Sorrow: A Theology of Philippians, Chris Bruno

Hidden with Christ in God: A Theology of Colossians and Philemon, Kevin W. McFadden

To Walk and to Please God: A Theology of 1 and 2 Thessalonians, Andrew S. Malone

The Appearing of God Our Savior: A Theology of 1 and 2 Timothy and Titus, Claire S. Smith

Perfect Priest for Weary Pilgrims: A Theology of Hebrews, Dennis E. Johnson

Living Faith: A Theology of James, Robert L. Plummer

The God Who Judges and Saves: A Theology of 2 Peter and Jude, Matthew S. Harmon

The Joy of Hearing: A Theology of the Book of Revelation, Thomas R. Schreiner

"There is obviously great value in working through a book like Romans from beginning to end, chapter by chapter, and verse by verse (what we might call a 'longitudinal' approach). But a complementary 'latitudinal' approach that outlines the key theological themes of Romans is also important. Brian Rosner's book takes this second approach. It is the best available survey of the theology of this important and influential biblical book."

Douglas J. Moo, Professor of Biblical Studies Emeritus, Wheaton College; author, *The Letter to the Romans* (New International Commentary on the New Testament)

"This is a wonderful introduction to Romans! It is clear, concise, and peppered with insights that come from a careful study of the letter itself and the best secondary literature on it. Preachers, teachers, students, and anyone interested in Romans will benefit from reading the letter in tandem with this helpful guide to its riches."

Frank Thielman, Presbyterian Chair of Divinity, Beeson Divinity School; author, *Romans* (Zondervan Exegetical Commentary on the New Testament)

"The church today struggles with massive questions concerning how to live and think Christianly in a world such as ours. Brian Rosner's crystal-clear, careful overview of the theology of the book of Romans can help. Rosner's little book is both thorough, covering key topics of the letter, and admirably efficient. Unpacking the apostle's message in an orderly fashion, Rosner shows how Christ followers might be strengthened in the face of world forces that would deform and weaken us. We need gospel strength, so we desperately need to hear Romans afresh, and this book helps us do just that."

George H. Guthrie, Professor of New Testament, Regent College, Vancouver

"Everyone likes to receive a present! Paul wrote his famous letter to explain and apply the gospel to his Roman readers. That clearer understanding of the gospel is described by Paul as his 'spiritual gift' to the church (Rom. 1:11). What better gift can be imagined than to be helped to properly understand the message of the gospel. Rosner's book is like wrapping paper around this precious gift that is the message of Romans, helping us to recognize Romans as a good gift. He shows that Romans is best read through the double lens of the key motifs of the gospel and righteousness."

Gregory Goswell, Honorary Research Fellow, Christ College, Sydney, Australia

"*Strengthened by the Gospel* is undoubtedly a volume that many seminary students, pastors, and lay leaders will want on their bookshelves. It is clearly the fruit of many years of study in Romans, written with clarity and depth. The big theological themes of the letter are supported by well-crafted arguments based on familiarity with the granular details of Romans. All will benefit richly from Rosner's devotion to the text and theology of Romans."

M. Sydney Park, Associate Professor of Divinity, Beeson Divinity School

"Brian Rosner has been studying, teaching, and meditating on Paul's incredibly rich and powerful letter to the Romans for many years. He is both an extraordinarily gifted exegete and an incredibly insightful theologian with a special expertise in biblical theology. All of that is on full display in this masterful exposition of the theology of Paul's letter to the Romans. All who read it will not only grow to a deeper understanding of Romans and its theology but will also be spiritually edified and enriched in the process. Rosner sets the table so that we can all more fully enjoy the theological feast of Paul's letter to the Romans."

Roy E. Ciampa, Professor Emeritus of Biblical and Religious Studies, Samford University

"*Strengthened by the Gospel* blends biblical theology and pastoral insight into a rich reading of Romans from a master teacher. Brian Rosner compellingly holds forth the gospel as the center of Paul's argument and, in so doing, illuminates the theological message of Romans while remaining ever attentive to its practical implications. This book is an invaluable resource for preachers and students alike, providing both clarity and depth as it integrates the various elements of Romans. Readers will come away strengthened in their grasp of how the gospel shapes the Christian's mind, heart, and conduct."

Philip H. Kern, Head of New Testament, Moore Theological College

Strengthened by the Gospel

A Theology of Romans

Brian S. Rosner

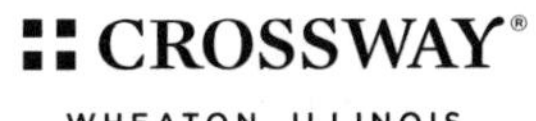

WHEATON, ILLINOIS

Strengthened by the Gospel: A Theology of Romans

Published by Crossway
1300 Crescent Street
Wheaton, Illinois 60187

Cover design: Kevin Lipp

First printing 2025

Printed in the United States of America

All emphases in Scripture quotations have been added by the author.

Trade paperback ISBN: 978-1-4335-7255-5
ePub ISBN: 978-1-4335-7257-9
PDF ISBN: 978-1-4335-7256-2

Library of Congress Cataloging-in-Publication Data

Names: Rosner, Brian S., author.
Title: Strengthened by the gospel : a theology of Romans / Brian S. Rosner.
Description: Wheaton, Illinois : Crossway, [2025] | Series: New Testament theology | Includes bibliographical references and index.
Identifiers: LCCN 2024038808 (print) | LCCN 2024038809 (ebook) | ISBN 9781433572555 (trade paperback) | ISBN 9781433572562 (pdf) | ISBN 9781433572579 (epub)
Subjects: LCSH: Bible. Romans—Theology.
Classification: LCC BS2665.52 .R66 2025 (print) | LCC BS2665.52 (ebook) | DDC 227/.106—dc23/eng/20250416
LC record available at https://lccn.loc.gov/2024038808
LC ebook record available at https://lccn.loc.gov/2024038809

Crossway is a publishing ministry of Good News Publishers.

VP 34 33 32 31 30 29 28 27 26 25
15 14 13 12 11 10 9 8 7 6 5 4 3 2 1

To
Jitto and Shyamala Arulampalam
Conrad and Theresa Chui
Greg and Beth Hammond
David and Carol Knox
Andrew and Kathryn Thorburn

Contents

Tables

Series Preface

THERE ARE REMARKABLY FEW TREATMENTS of the big ideas of single books of the New Testament. Readers can find brief coverage in Bible dictionaries, in some commentaries, and in New Testament theologies, but such books are filled with other information and are not devoted to unpacking the theology of each New Testament book in its own right. Technical works concentrating on various themes of New Testament theology often have a narrow focus, treating some aspect of the teaching of, say, Matthew or Hebrews in isolation from the rest of the book's theology.

The New Testament Theology series seeks to fill this gap by providing students of Scripture with readable book-length treatments of the distinctive teaching of each New Testament book or collection of books. The volumes approach the text from the perspective of biblical theology. They pay due attention to the historical and literary dimensions of the text, but their main focus is on presenting the teaching of particular New Testament books about God and his relations to the world on their own terms, maintaining sight of the Bible's overarching narrative and Christocentric focus. Such biblical theology is of fundamental importance to biblical and expository preaching and informs exegesis, systematic theology, and Christian ethics.

The twenty volumes in the series supply comprehensive, scholarly, and accessible treatments of theological themes from an evangelical perspective. We envision them being of value to students, preachers, and interested laypeople. When preparing an expository sermon series, for example, pastors can find a healthy supply of informative commentaries, but there are few options for coming to terms with the overall teaching of each book of the New Testament. As well as being useful in sermon and Bible study preparation, the volumes will also be of value as textbooks in college and seminary exegesis classes. Our prayer is that they contribute to a deeper understanding of and commitment to the kingdom and glory of God in Christ.

Virtually all agree that Romans represents the fullest expression of the Pauline gospel, and thus we must attend to Romans if we desire to understand Pauline theology. Brian Rosner takes us on a remarkably comprehensive yet compact tour of the theology of this beautiful and amazing letter. The gospel Paul proclaimed includes the plight and fallenness of human beings and the love of God in Jesus Christ's death and resurrection that justifies, redeems, and reconciles those who put their faith in Christ. Those who are saved by the grace of God are empowered by the Spirit to live new lives where love marks out the church as God's people. At the same time, the transformed lives of believers bear witness to the world. Believers are strengthened and encouraged by the gospel, and thus we have an unshakeable hope that encourages and fortifies us.

Thomas R. Schreiner and Brian S. Rosner

Preface

WHEN THE OPPORTUNITY AROSE to join Tom Schreiner as coeditor of a series of books on New Testament theology, I took a deep breath and volunteered to write the volume on Romans. I have been teaching and writing about Romans for thirty-five years, and as a follower of Jesus Christ I have been repeatedly edified and nourished by its message. But writing about Romans is not only a great blessing but also an enormous challenge. Paul's longest letter is also his most studied and complex. Romans ranks among the most influential letters ever written, having exercised a profound effect on countless lives and many societies for two thousand years.

Despite my familiarity with its contents, I learned much about Paul's most magisterial letter in writing this book. Romans not only trumpets the grace of God in the gospel but also contains life-giving teaching about the benefits of the gospel, the nature of evil, the good life, the praise and worship of God, the human mind, healthy Christian living, how to disagree agreeably, the life and work of Jesus, the power of the Holy Spirit, and much more. To read Romans for all its worth, I found the letter opening and closing to be critical. Of equal importance is the discipline of reading the letter cumulatively, not missing the theological wood for the exegetical trees. Most of all, I learned that the gospel of God is not just for non-Christians but is God's primary means of strengthening believers in Christ.

I am deeply grateful to many people for their support and encouragement along the way. Most of the work was completed on a generous study leave provided by Ridley College. A number of friends read and commented helpfully on drafts of the book: Bryan Blazosky, Tricia Blazosky, Roy Ciampa, Frank Szanto, and my wonderful wife, Natalie. Mark Simon cowrote an article with me on the purpose of Romans that was a turning point in my understanding of the letter. Peter Williams, my excellent and longsuffering PA, provided able assistance at many stages. Chris Cowan's work as editor was exemplary and made many improvements. It is a privilege to work with Tom Schreiner, Justin Taylor, and the team at Crossway. *Strengthened by the Gospel* is dedicated to a choice group of friends who support my work of research and writing.

Writing the book has left me more convinced than ever that the gospel of God has the power to bring joy, peace, and hope to all who welcome its message.

Abbreviations

AB	Anchor Bible
BDAG	Danker, Frederick W., Walter Bauer, William F. Arndt, and F. Wilbur Gingrich, eds., *Greek-English Lexicon of the New Testament and Other Early Christian Literature*. 3rd ed. Chicago: University of Chicago Press, 2000.
BECNT	Baker Exegetical Commentary on the New Testament
BNTC	Black's New Testament Commentary
BTCP	Biblical Theology for Christian Proclamation
BTFL	Biblical Theology for Life
BTNT	Biblical Theology of the New Testament
BZNW	Beihefte zur Zeitschrift für die neutestamentliche Wissenschaft
CNTUOT	*Commentary on the New Testament Use of the Old Testament*. Edited by G. K. Beale and D. A. Carson. Grand Rapids, MI: Baker Academic, 2007.
DNTUOT	*Dictionary of the New Testament Use of the Old Testament*. Edited by G. K. Beale, D. A. Carson, Benjamin L. Gladd, and Andrew David Naselli. Grand Rapids, MI: Baker Academic, 2023.
DPL	*Dictionary of Paul and His Letters*. Edited by G. F. Hawthorne, R. P. Martin, and D. G. Reid. Downers Grove, IL: InterVarsity Press, 1993.

DPL[2]	*Dictionary of Paul and His Letters*, 2nd ed. Edited by Scot McKnight. Downers Grove, IL: IVP Academic, 2023.
EGGNT	Exegetical Guide to the Greek New Testament
ESVEC	*ESV Expository Commentary*
ExpTim	*Expository Times*
FET	Foundations of Evangelical Theology
ICC	International Critical Commentary
Int	*Interpretation*
JETS	*Journal of the Evangelical Theological Society*
JSNT	*Journal for the Study of the New Testament*
JSNTSup	Journal for the Study of the New Testament Supplement Series
JTS	*Journal of Theological Studies*
L&N	Louw, Johannes P., and Eugene A. Nida, eds. *Greek–English Lexicon of the New Testament: Based on Semantic Domains*. New York: United Bible Societies, 1996.
LNTS	The Library of New Testament Studies
LXX	Septuagint
NDBT	*New Dictionary of Biblical Theology*. Edited by T. D. Alexander and B. S. Rosner. Downers Grove, IL: InterVarsity Press, 2000.
NIB	*The New Interpreter's Bible*. Edited by Leander E. Keck. 12 vols. Nashville: Abingdon, 1994–2004.
NICNT	New International Commentary on the New Testament
NIGTC	New International Greek Testament Commentary
NSBT	New Studies in Biblical Theology
NTS	*New Testament Studies*
OTP	*Old Testament Pseudepigrapha*. Edited by James H. Charlesworth. 2 vols. New York: Doubleday, 1983, 1985.
PNTC	Pillar New Testament Commentary
RevExp	*Review and Expositor*
SGBC	The Story of God Bible Commentary
SNTSMS	Society for New Testament Studies Monograph Series

TDNT	*Theological Dictionary of the New Testament*. Edited by Gerhard Kittel and Gerhard Friedrich. Translated by Geoffrey W. Bromiley. 10 vols. Grand Rapids, MI: Eerdmas, 1964–76.
UBS[4]	*The Greek New Testament*. Edited by B. Aland, K. Aland, J. Karavidopoulos, C. M. Martini, and B. M. Metzger. 4th rev. ed. Stuttgart: Deutsche Bibelgesellschaft: United Bible Societies, 1993.
WBC	Word Biblical Commentary
WUNT	Wissenschaftliche Untersuchungen zum Neuen Testament
ZECNT	Zondervan Exegetical Commentary on the New Testament

Introduction

The Purpose of Romans

Eager to preach the gospel.

ROMANS 1:15

THE BOOK OF ROMANS plumbs the depths of human sin and evil and then tells the ultimate good-news story about how God transforms all of human life and history. No book in the Bible explains more fully the amazing love of God in the gospel of the Lord Jesus Christ and its impact on our lives and world. For those who believe its message, Romans promises that the God of hope will fill them with joy and peace, causing them to overflow with hope by the power of the Holy Spirit (Rom. 15:13). Romans richly repays repeated reading and careful study.

The first step in reading Romans for all its worth is to understand Paul's purpose in writing. Why did Paul write this letter? And how does his purpose in writing it affect the way that we read it today?

The purpose of Romans has long been debated, ramping up since the mid-twentieth century. The many proposals that have been offered prioritize various sections of the letter. For example, in broad terms, the Reformation approach sees the teaching on justification by faith as critical and views Romans 1–8 as the most significant section of the letter. In contrast the new perspective on Paul yields a strong focus on Romans 9–11. Recently, a pastoral hypothesis suggesting that Romans was occasioned by Paul's desire to settle a dispute between Christians from Jewish and Gentile backgrounds gives Romans 12–15 pride of place.

However, Pauline letters typically reveal their themes and major concerns in the epistolary frame—in the opening greetings and thanksgiving and in the letter closing. These sections of Romans provide explicit indicators of Paul's reasons for writing. Jeffrey Weima highlights how Romans 1:1–7 stresses "the legitimacy of Paul's apostleship and trustworthiness of his gospel"[1] and his desire to incorporate the Roman Gentile Christians into his apostolic sphere.[2] The thanksgiving in 1:8–15 emphasizes Paul's apostolic obligation to foster the Roman Christians' growth in faith and to impart a spiritual gift to them. The final chapters of Romans include a description of Paul's mission and future plans (15:14–32) and a closing (15:33–16:27), both of which function to cultivate the Roman Christians' acceptance of Paul's apostolic authority over them and the gospel he has presented to them in the body of the letter.[3]

Indeed, a good case can be made for the gospel as the main theme of the letter. The word "gospel" (*euangelion*) appears twice in the letter opening (1:1, 9) and twice in its closing (15:16, 19), and the verb "to preach the gospel" (*euangelizō*) occurs once in each (1:15; 15:20). The gospel is also the subject of what is widely regarded as the thesis statement of Romans (1:16–17). Paul writes as one who is "set apart for the gospel of God" (1:1), is in the "priestly service of the gospel of God" (15:16), and is "eager to preach the gospel . . . in Rome" (1:15). He opens the body of the letter with the declaration "I am not ashamed of the gospel" (1:16).

If "Romans is an exposition of the gospel and its many implications,"[4] what did Paul hope to achieve by presenting his gospel to people who

1 Jeffrey A. D. Weima, "The Reason for Romans: The Evidence of Its Epistolary Framework (1:1–15; 15:14–16:27)," *RevExp* 100, no. 1 (2003): 20.

2 Jeffrey A. D. Weima, *Paul the Ancient Letter Writer: An Introduction to Epistolary Analysis* (Grand Rapids, MI: Baker Academic, 2016), 18–19.

3 Weima, "The Reason for Romans," 25, 30.

4 David G. Peterson, *Commentary on Romans*, BTCP (Nashville: Holman Reference, 2017), 50.

had already responded positively to it—namely, to the Christians in Rome (1:7)? After all, Paul himself states, "I make it my ambition to preach the gospel, not where Christ has already been named" (15:20).

A common answer to this question is that Paul wrote the letter with missionary and apologetic purposes. The missionary purpose is clear in Romans 15. Paul informs the Roman Christians of his desire to visit them on his way to preach the gospel and plant churches in Spain (15:23–24). Paul wanted to enlist their interest, prayers, and support: "I hope to see you in passing as I go to Spain, and to be helped on my journey [*propempō*] there by you" (15:24).[5] Just as Syrian Antioch was Paul's home base for his first three missionary journeys in the east of the Roman Empire, so also Paul apparently hoped that Rome would become a base for his missions farther west. In this sense Romans is a letter of introduction in which Paul explains both his message and agenda fairly comprehensively (see 15:14–24).

Romans also functions as an apology for Paul, the sort of defense he would soon be giving in Judea when he brought the money he had been collecting from the Gentile churches to Jerusalem for the poor Jewish believers (see 15:25–33). In presenting the gospel in Romans, Paul, who was familiar with opposition, wrote to defend both himself and his message.

Paul's Desire to Strengthen the Believers in Rome

Paul's purpose in presenting the gospel in Romans was not only to enlist the support of the Roman Christians for his gospel mission in Rome and beyond and to defend that same gospel and mission from potential misunderstandings and opponents but also to benefit his readers themselves. Two texts in the letter frame make this clear.

Romans 1:11–15

In 1:11–15 Paul tells the Roman Christians what he would like to do for them when he visits them in person. "I long to see you . . . [and]

5 The verb "to be helped on a journey" is a technical term for material assistance—meaning, food and money. Cf. 1 Cor. 16:6, 11.

have often intended to come to you" (1:11, 13). To recognize the importance of this passage for understanding the purpose of Romans, we must remember that in the ancient world, letters regularly functioned as a substitute for the author's personal presence. In terms reminiscent of 1:11–15, Libanius, a teacher of rhetoric in the ancient world, wrote in one of his letters, "Now, it would be sweeter to be able to see one another, but neither is the second-best choice trivial, namely, to send and to receive a letter."[6] That Paul shares this perspective can be seen in 2 Corinthians 10:11 where, with reference to his apostolic authority, he writes, "Let such a person understand that what we say by letter when absent, we do when present." Similarly, in 1 Corinthians 5:3 Paul writes, "For though absent in body, I am present in spirit." It is safe to assume that Paul aims to accomplish in his letter at least part of what he hopes to achieve when visiting the Roman Christians in person.

> For I long to see you, *that I may impart to you some spiritual gift to strengthen you*—that is, *that we may be mutually encouraged by each other's faith*, both yours and mine. I do not want you to be unaware, brothers, that I have often intended to come to you (but thus far have been prevented), *in order that I may reap some harvest among you as well as among the rest of the Gentiles*. I am under obligation both to Greeks and to barbarians, both to the wise and to the foolish. So *I am eager to preach the gospel to you also who are in Rome*. (Rom. 1:11–15)

Three times in this passage Paul mentions his desire to come to Rome to see the Christians there in person (1:11, 13, 15). He gives four reasons for wanting to do so (1:11, 12, 13, 15; see the italicized words above): to impart a spiritual gift to them, to experience mutual encouragement, to reap a harvest among them, and to preach the gospel to them.

6 Scott Bradbury, *Selected Letters of Libanius: From the Age of Constantius and Julian*, Translated Texts for Historians 41 (Liverpool: Liverpool University Press, 2004), 66 (37.4). Cf. Libanius, *Autobiography and Selected Letters, Volume I: Autobiography. Letters 1–50*, ed. and trans. A. F. Norman, LCL 478 (Cambridge, MA: Harvard University Press, 1992), 22: "When you look at my letter, think that you are looking at me" (letter 245.9 quoted in the introduction).

The first and last reasons in Romans 1:11 and 1:15 are subject to different interpretations. Some take the "spiritual gift" that Paul wants to impart to the Christians in Rome to be the sort of spiritual gifts he lists in Romans 12:6–8 and 1 Corinthians 12:1–4, 7–11, 28.[7] However, the combination of words that Paul uses for "spiritual gift" in Romans 1:11—"spiritual" (*pneumatikos)* and "gift" (*charisma*)—is not his usual way of referring to "the spiritual gifts." In Romans 12:6; 1 Corinthians 1:7; and 12:4, he refers just to "gifts" (*charismata*). In 1 Corinthians 12:1 he uses "spiritual things" (*tōn pneumatikōn*), which is usually translated "spiritual gifts" in light of the context of 1 Corinthians 12–14. In addition, Paul makes clear in 1 Corinthians 12:6–7 that *God* imparts the gifts of the Spirit; nowhere in his letters does Paul envisage a human being bestowing a spiritual gift.

It is more likely that the spiritual gift Paul wants to impart is his understanding of the gospel. The beginning and end of the paragraph—Romans 1:11 and 15—essentially say the same thing: Paul wants to strengthen the Roman Christians by imparting to them the spiritual gift of his preaching the gospel to them. This will result in reaping a "[spiritual] harvest" among them (Rom. 1:13), an image reminiscent of 1 Corinthians 9:11 where Paul refers to preaching the gospel as having "sown spiritual seed" (NIV). Thomas Schreiner writes, "The gift mentioned here [in Rom. 1:11] relates directly to the purpose of the Roman Letter. The Roman Christians need to understand the Pauline gospel . . . an apostolic gift, which is communicated in this letter."[8]

While it is true that Paul normally uses the verb "to preach the gospel" to refer to his proclamation of the good news to unbelievers, it would be a mistake to conclude that he believes that gospel preaching brings no benefits to those who have already believed. We should take Paul's desire to preach the gospel in 1:15 in the broad sense of both evangelizing the lost and building up the saints in Rome. Immediately

7 E.g., C. K. Barrett, *The Epistle to the Romans*, rev. ed., BNTC (London: Continuum, 1991), 25–26.

8 Thomas R. Schreiner, *Romans*, 2nd ed., BECNT (Grand Rapids, MI: Baker Academic, 2018), 59–60.

following 1:15, Paul launches into an exposition of the gospel ("For I am not ashamed of the gospel," 1:16), and "he is not done until the epistle is at an end."[9]

As Douglas Moo states, the gospel has "a broad range of significance in Paul. It is, of course, the instrument that God uses to bring people into the new realm. But it is also the instrument that God uses to produce growth in those who already know Christ."[10] Colin Kruse is right that Paul "believed his explanation of the gospel, when understood by his audience, would make them strong in their faith."[11]

Romans 16:25–26

"Now to him who is able to strengthen you according to my gospel and the preaching of Jesus Christ, according to the revelation of the mystery that was kept secret for long ages but has now been disclosed and through the prophetic writings has been made known to all nations" (Rom. 16:25–26).

This text, the first lines of the letter's closing doxology, is an inclusio with the opening of the letter.[12] Specifically, "my gospel, that is to say, the preaching about Jesus Christ" (16:25 my translation)[13] recalls Paul's assertion in 1:2 that the gospel he preaches concerns God's Son, Jesus Christ. And Paul's gospel being rooted in the "prophetic writings [*graphōn prophētikōn*]" (16:26) of the Old Testament echoes Paul's words in 1:2 that the gospel was "promised beforehand through his [God's] prophets [*tōn prophētōn*] in the holy Scriptures [*graphais*]."

Paul's hope that God would "strengthen" the Christians in Rome (16:25) takes us back to 1:11, the only other use of the verb *stērizō* in the letter. Here Paul hopes to strengthen the Roman Christians with

9 Barrett, *The Epistle to the Romans*, 27.

10 Douglas J. Moo, *A Theology of Paul and His Letters: The Gift of the New Realm in Christ*, BTNT (Grand Rapids, MI: Zondervan Academic, 2021), 51.

11 Colin G. Kruse, *Paul's Letter to the Romans*, PNTC (Grand Rapids, MI: Eerdmans, 2012), 66.

12 Cf. Jeffrey A. D. Weima, *Neglected Endings: The Significance of the Pauline Letter Closings*, JSNTSup 101 (Edinburgh: T&T Clark, 1994), 219: "The doxology is, in fact, especially striking for the way in which it recapitulates the concern of Paul evident in the epistolary framework of the letter."

13 The conjunction *kai* is epexegetical and "of Jesus Christ" is an objective genitive.

the spiritual gift of his preaching the gospel of Jesus Christ to them (1:11, 15). God strengthens believers "according to [*kata*] my gospel" (16:25)—that is, the strength is based on the gospel and comes through the gospel.[14] Paul is effectively saying, May God strengthen you through the gospel that I have just presented in this letter, which is a substitute for what I had hoped to do if I could have come and visited.

As it turns out, the goal of strengthening (*stērizō*) believers with the gospel is a good description of what Paul seeks to do for those who have already come to faith in Christ. Apart from the two occurrences in Romans, Paul uses the verb "to strengthen" four times in his letters:

> We sent Timothy, our brother and co-worker for God in proclaiming the gospel of Christ, to *strengthen* and encourage you. (1 Thess. 3:2 NRSV)

> Now may our God and Father himself . . . so *strengthen* your hearts in holiness that you may be blameless before our God and Father at the coming of our Lord Jesus with all his saints. (1 Thess. 3:11, 13 NRSV)

> Now may our Lord Jesus Christ himself and God our Father, who loved us and through grace gave us eternal comfort and good hope, comfort your hearts and *strengthen* them in every good work and word. (2 Thess. 2:16–17 NRSV)

> But the Lord is faithful; he will *strengthen* you and guard you from the evil one. (2 Thess. 3:3 NRSV)

In these texts, God is the one who strengthens, encourages, and comforts believers with the gospel of Christ, thereby equipping them for every good work and word so that they may live holy lives, protected from the evil one. It is no coincidence that Paul's presentation of the gospel in Romans strengthens believers in many of the same ways.

14 Cf. Schreiner, *Romans*, 785, commenting on the preposition *kata* in 16:25.

Remarkably, Acts records a similar agenda for Paul's visits to churches that were already established. The four occurrences of the verb "to strengthen"—*epistērizō*, a compound form of *stērizō*—are used in contexts where Paul and his coworkers strengthen believers:

> When they [Paul and Barnabas] had preached the gospel to that city [Derbe] and had made many disciples, they returned to Lystra and to Iconium and to Antioch, *strengthening the souls of the disciples, encouraging them to continue in the faith.* (Acts 14:21–22)

> And Judas and Silas, who were themselves prophets, *encouraged and strengthened the brothers with many words.* (Acts 15:32)

> And he [Paul] went through Syria and Cilicia, *strengthening the churches.* (Acts 15:41)

> After spending some time there [in Antioch], he [Paul] departed and went from one place to the next through the region of Galatia and Phrygia, *strengthening all the disciples.* (Acts 18:23)

When Paul and his coworkers ministered to people who had already heard and believed the gospel, they sought to strengthen and encourage them with many words to continue in the faith.

The Purpose of Romans

The thesis of this book, based on the letter frame and the usage of key terms elsewhere in the New Testament, is that Paul wrote Romans not only to defend his apostolic authority and to enlist the support of the Roman Christians for his mission but also to strengthen his readers with a full presentation of his gospel.

Ann Jervis's structural analysis of Romans also focuses on the opening and closing chapters of the letter and comes to a similar conclusion. She seeks to incorporate Paul's explicitly stated goal in 15:24 of making Rome a base from which to launch his mission to Spain (the missiological purpose of Romans) with the theological purpose of gospel proclamation and apostolic incorporation.[15] In particular, she highlights 15:16, which portrays Paul's ministry to the Gentiles as "priestly service of the gospel of God, so that the offering of the Gentiles may be acceptable, sanctified by the Holy Spirit." Jervis concludes,

> The function of Romans is to encourage the Roman believers to enter Paul's apostolic orbit so that they may be included within his "offering" through having heard his preaching. . . . Romans is written to fulfil Paul's mandate to establish and nurture his Roman readers in a life of faith marked by obedience and holiness—to preach the gospel to them.[16]

Paul writes to the Christians in Rome not only as apostle and missionary but also as pastor.

The idea that Paul wrote Romans with a pastoral purpose has grown in popularity in recent years. Many scholars read between the lines of Romans 14:1–15:13 and infer that the Roman Christian community was split between Jewish and Gentile factions. In this light, Romans is not a general treatise on Paul's theology but, rather, occasional in nature (like his other letters), addressing specific concerns in the church. The first part of Romans, then, is seen as presenting a theology that bolsters Paul's plea that the two groups "accept one another" (15:7 NIV); and Jew-Gentile relationships are seen as prominent throughout the letter, reaching center stage in Romans 9–11.

This reading of Romans is, however, open to critique. John Barclay and Nijay Gupta have provided some objective criteria by which to test such mirror readings of Paul's letters.[17] Applying those tests to Romans

15 L. Ann Jervis, *The Purpose of Romans: A Comparative Letter Structure Investigation*, JSNTSup 55 (Sheffield: JSOT Press, 1991), 19, 126–27.

16 Jervis, *The Purpose of Romans*, 164.

17 John M. G. Barclay, "Mirror-Reading a Polemical Letter: Galatians as a Test Case," *JSNT* 10, no. 31 (1987): 73–93; Nijay K. Gupta, "Mirror-Reading Moral Issues in Paul's Letters," *JSNT* 34, no. 4 (2012): 361–81. See Brian S. Rosner and Mark Simon, "Not Reading Romans Backwards: A Critique of the Pastoral Purpose of Romans," *Trinity Journal* (forthcoming), where

demonstrates that it has in fact a greater concern, for example, about holiness and sexual immorality (see Rom. 2, 6–8, 12) than about Jew-Gentile disunity. Furthermore, the omission of any mention of healing intra-church divisions in the epistolary frame is a strong indicator that the pastoral concerns of 14:1–15:13 do not constitute the major reason for Romans. Romans is an occasional letter, but the occasion has more to do with Paul than the Roman Christians. Whereas we would be left to speculation and conjecture if problems in the church occasioned the letter, Paul's situation and reasons for writing Romans are clear in the epistolary frame of the letter.

Paul does have a pastoral concern for the Roman Christians, but it is much broader than simply shoring up the unity of the church in Rome. Paul intends to strengthen the believers in Rome by fully proclaiming the gospel of Christ to them. My task in this book is to study the theology of Romans, setting forth the shape and scope of Paul's gospel and its many implications with the same goal of strengthening and encouraging disciples of Jesus in our day.

The Place of Romans in the New Testament Canon

In English Bibles, following the order of the Vulgate, Romans appears after Acts and as the first of Paul's letters.[a] The venerable status of this arrangement is borne out by the early manuscript evidence, much of which adheres to this order.[b] While the text of Romans itself is primary for its interpretation, reading Romans in the light of its place in the canon is a legitimate and valuable complementary way of reading the letter.[c]

A close connection between Acts and Romans is suggested by the fact that Acts ends with Paul in Rome (28:11–31) and

---

we consider the works of Paul Minear, Francis Watson, and Scot McKnight, who advocate a narrow, pastoral purpose in Romans in terms of bringing unity to a divided church.

in Romans Paul writes to the saints in Rome (1:7) and reports his desire to visit Rome (1:8–15; 15:22–29). Indeed, reading Romans after Acts highlights themes that are central to both, most clearly the universal reach of the gospel of God's grace that is attested by the Old Testament. This can be seen in connection with several textual links:

1. Paul's pattern in Acts 13–28 is to take the gospel to Jews first and then turn to the Gentiles after the Jews had rejected the message. The same priorities are evident throughout Romans, beginning with the assertion that the "the gospel . . . is the power of God for salvation to everyone who believes, to the Jew first and also to the Greek" (1:16) and culminating in Romans 9–11 where Paul treats at length the problem and consequences of Jewish unbelief.
2. In the closing scene of Acts, Paul testifies (*diamarturomai*) "about Jesus both from the Law of Moses and from the Prophets" (Acts 28:23). In Romans Paul demonstrates that "the Law and the Prophets bear witness [*martureō*]" (Rom. 3:21) to the gospel he preaches (see chapter 6 below).
3. In both Acts 28:26–27 and Romans 11:11, Paul quotes Isaiah 6:9–10 to support his contention that the Old Testament prophesies Jewish rejection of Jesus.
4. In Acts 21:28 Jews accuse Paul of "teaching everyone everywhere against the people and the law and this place [i.e., the temple]." "Romans can be read as a canonical answer to these false charges,"[d] with its extensive treatments of the themes of the people of God, the law, and the temple—often in a polemical context.

Reading Romans prior to 1 Corinthians is a fitting way to introduce 1 Corinthians. Romans 15:14–21 represents Paul's most extensive account of how he conceives of his ministry as apostle to the Gentiles. He describes himself as "a minister of Christ Jesus to the Gentiles in the priestly service of the gospel of God, so that the offering of the Gentiles may be acceptable, sanctified by the Holy Spirit" (Rom. 15:16). This framing of Paul's gospel work in priestly and purity terms, themes that reverberate throughout Romans, corresponds to how Paul describes the Corinthian Christians in his letter opening: "To the church of God that is in Corinth, to those sanctified in Christ Jesus, called to be saints together with all those who in every place call upon the name of our Lord Jesus Christ, both their Lord and ours" (1 Cor. 1:2). Three times Paul stresses their holy status: They belong to God ("of God," a possessive genitive), are sanctified, and are called to be saints. The purity theme is then carried further in the letter, with Paul on two occasions describing the Corinthian Christians as God's temple (1 Cor. 3:16–17; 6:19–20).[e]

The letter to the Romans functions well as the head of the entire Pauline corpus, given its general nature in comparison with the other Pauline letters and its comprehensive presentation of Paul's gospel. The textual history of Romans supports this observation: Some early manuscripts of the letter omit "in Rome" in 1:7 and 15, a deletion that Metzger suggests was "made in order to show that the letter is of general, not local application."[f] Perhaps for similar reasons, the lengthy greetings to the Christians in Rome in Romans 16 are also omitted in some manuscripts. J. B. Lightfoot even suggests that Paul himself made the changes "to give his letter a wider circulation."[g]

Brevard Childs contends that "the placing of Romans as an introduction [to the Pauline corpus] was not a tour de force, but was encouraged by the very nature of the letter itself."[h] As Gregory Goswell puts it, Romans is "the most treatise-like of Paul's letters, and so it appropriately functions as a theological introduction to the Pauline corpus."[i] As such, *Paul's letters that follow Romans may be read as the contextual application of Paul's gospel, as presented in Romans, to the task of building up and strengthening churches.*[j] This way of reading Romans in its canonical setting fits well with the purpose and function of Romans defended in this introduction.

a Paul's letters are roughly in the order of longest to shortest, with (1) letters to the same churches kept together and (2) letters to churches before letters to individuals. Nonetheless, the reasons for the arrangement would have soon become irrelevant since readers would experience the effects of that order regardless of the reasons behind it. Either way, the presentation gives Romans a certain priority.

b Gregory Goswell, "Reading Romans after the Book of Acts," *JETS* 62, no. 2 (2019): 354. The canonical context of Romans varies with the manuscript tradition. Sometimes the Pauline Epistles are found by themselves, and Romans typically stands as the start of the corpus. It is also common in Greek manuscripts to find that Romans comes after the Catholic Epistles, which come after Acts.

c See Gregory Goswell, *Text and Paratext: Book Order, Title, and Division as Keys to Biblical Interpretation* (Bellingham, WA: Lexham Academic, 2023), for an introduction to the significance of paratextual features for biblical interpretation, including the order of the books in the canon.

d Goswell, "Reading Romans," 369.

e See further Roy Ciampa and Brian Rosner, "The Structure and Argument of 1 Corinthians: A Biblical/Jewish Approach," *NTS* 52, no. 2 (2006): 205–18; Brian Rosner, "The Church as Temple and Moral Exhortation in 1 Corinthians," in *Ecclesia and Ethics: Moral Formation and the Church*, ed. E. Allan Jones III, John Frederick, John Anthony Dunne, Eric Lewellen, and Janghoon Park (London: Bloomsbury T&T Clark, 2016), 41–54.

f Bruce Manning Metzger, *A Textual Commentary on the Greek New Testament*, 2nd ed. (New York: United Bible Societies, 1994), 446.

g J. B. Lightfoot, *Biblical Essays* (London: MacMillan, 1904), 319.

h Brevard Childs, *The Church's Guide for Reading Paul: The Canonical Shaping of the Pauline Corpus* (Grand Rapids, MI: Eerdmans, 2008), 175.

i Gregory Goswell, "The Bookends of the Pauline Corpus," *JETS* 65, no. 1 (2022): 115.

j Unsurprisingly, many treatments of Paul's theology in his letters give pride of place to Romans. E.g., James D. G. Dunn uses Romans as the foundation for his exposition of Paul's entire theology: Romans "is the most sustained and reflective statement of Paul's own theology by Paul himself." James D. G. Dunn, *The Theology of Paul the Apostle* (Grand Rapids, MI: Eerdmans, 1998), 25.

1

A Theology of Romans

The gospel of God.

ROMANS 1:1; 15:16

IF PAUL'S MAIN PURPOSE in Romans is to strengthen the Roman Christians with the gospel, what is the gospel according to Romans? In this chapter we begin an investigation of what Romans teaches about the gospel of God, setting the course for the rest of this book.

The Gospel in Romans

Paul does not often define the gospel in his letters, perhaps because most of his letters are written to churches or individuals that have heard Paul preach the gospel in person.[1] Five passages stand out as succinct but partial descriptions of the good news, three of which are in Romans: 1:1–6; 1:16–17; 16:25–27. The other two are 1 Corinthians 15:1–8 and Galatians 3:7–9.

The two passages in Romans 1 are best taken as complementary, given their proximity to one another. Whereas 1:1–6 focuses on the content of the gospel (i.e., Jesus Christ),[2] 1:16–17 explains its main

1 The only exceptions are Romans and Colossians.

2 In 10:16–17, "the gospel . . . [is] the word of Christ," an objective genitive meaning "the message about Christ."

functions (i.e., to reveal the righteousness of God and to save everyone who believes). The third text, 16:25–27, as noted in the introduction, is effectively a restatement of the first.

> Paul, a servant of Christ Jesus, called to be an apostle, set apart for the gospel of God, which he promised beforehand through his prophets in the holy Scriptures, concerning his Son, who was descended from David according to the flesh and was declared to be the Son of God in power according to the Spirit of holiness by his resurrection from the dead, Jesus Christ our Lord, through whom we have received grace and apostleship to bring about the obedience of faith for the sake of his name among all the nations, including you who are called to belong to Jesus Christ. (Rom. 1:1–6)

> For I am not ashamed of the gospel, for it is the power of God for salvation to everyone who believes, to the Jew first and also to the Greek. For in it the righteousness of God is revealed from faith for faith, as it is written, "The righteous shall live by faith." (Rom. 1:16–17)

> Now to him who is able to strengthen you according to my gospel and the preaching of Jesus Christ, according to the revelation of the mystery that was kept secret for long ages but has now been disclosed and through the prophetic writings has been made known to all nations, according to the command of the eternal God, to bring about the obedience of faith—to the only wise God be glory forevermore through Jesus Christ! Amen. (Rom. 16:25–27)

Notwithstanding their incomplete and selective nature, the three passages form a handy introduction to the main contours of the gospel as Paul presents it in Romans. The gospel is the "gospel of God" (1:1; cf. 15:16).[3] It comes from God and is about God, revealing his

3 Commentators disagree whether the phrase is a genitive of source or an objective genitive. The following verse (1:2) indicates that the gospel was promised by God (a divine

power, righteousness (1:16–17), and wisdom (16:27). Its content is Christologically focused: the identity of Jesus Christ as the powerful "Son of God" and "Lord" (1:4) and "his resurrection from the dead" (1:4).[4] The gospel's main function is soteriological; it is "the power of God for salvation" (1:16). The gospel is no novel innovation but represents the fulfilment of prophetic promises (1:2–3, 17; 16:26); it has a universal reach, including "all the nations" (1:5), both Jews and Gentiles (1:16). It calls for "the obedience of faith" (1:5; 16:26). Those who respond in faith (the called) belong to Jesus Christ (1:6) and are declared righteous before God (1:16–17). (I will say more about each of these elements in other parts of the book.) In short, the gospel is a public announcement about Jesus Christ that saves those who respond in faith.

The partial nature of these gospel summaries in Romans is evident from the absence of three critical elements of Paul's presentation of the gospel that are covered in detail elsewhere in Romans: (1) the need for salvation, (2) the role of Christ's death and resurrection in securing our salvation, and (3) the blessings of salvation. All three are explicitly connected to the gospel in other parts of the letter. The judgment of God against human sin at the second coming of Christ ("on that day") is signalled in 2:16 as being "according to my [Paul's] gospel." In numerous passages the death of Christ achieves our salvation (e.g., 3:25; 5:6–7). And in 5:1–11 Paul declares that having been "justified by faith" (5:1) and "justified by his blood" (5:9) we have certain blessings: Believers have peace with God, have access to God, rejoice in their sufferings, are assured of God's love, can rest in hope, and receive the Holy Spirit.

The gospel of God is the work of God. According to Romans, we are saved not only by the grace of God (3:24; 4:16; 5:2, 15, 17, 20, 21; 6:1, 14, 15; 11:5, 6) but also because of his mercy (9:15, 16, 23; 11:30,

---

passive) in the Holy Scriptures, favoring a genitive of source. Either way, both meanings are clearly taught throughout Romans.

4 Cf. 2 Tim. 2:8: "Remember Jesus Christ, risen from the dead, the offspring of David, as preached in my gospel."

32; 12:1), kindness (2:4; 11:22), patience (2:4; 9:22), forbearance (2:4; 3:25), and love (1:7; 5:5, 8; 8:28, 35, 37, 39; 9:13, 25; 11:28; 12:19; 15:30).

In 1:7 Paul wishes the Roman Christians "grace" and "peace." These two words beautifully sum up Paul's gospel. *Grace* is God's beneficence and bounty, the cause of salvation; *peace* is the well-being and welfare of those who are saved, the outcome of salvation. When Paul offers a brief summary of Romans 1–4 in 5:1–2, it is no accident that he refers back to these two words: Having been justified by faith, we have *peace* with God and stand in *grace*.

The bulk of references to the gospel in Paul's letters refer to the offer of salvation to all people (cf. Eph. 1:13: "the gospel of your salvation"). However, as much as we treasure the assurance of personal salvation, we should also recognize that Paul's gospel "involves much more than the initial call of sinners to embrace Christ."[5] David Peterson writes,

> The apostle [in Romans] is not simply concerned about the way individuals may be justified by faith and escape final judgment. Rather, his aim is to explain how God's saving plan is to restore people from every nation to a right relationship with their Creator and with one another, ultimately to share in the glory of a redeemed creation.[6]

Beyond the personal, the gospel in Romans has ecclesial, apocalyptic, eschatological, and even cosmic dimensions.

Sometimes Paul's gospel of justification by faith in Romans is contrasted with Jesus's preaching "the gospel of the kingdom" (Matt. 4:23) in the Synoptic Gospels. However, the two are not at odds with each other; there are different ways in which to express the one gospel. Even in Romans, where Paul frames his gospel presentation in terms of righteousness and justification, kingdom language is present. Those who stand before the Lord justified (Rom. 14:4) are members of "the

5 Douglas J. Moo, *A Theology of Paul and His Letters: The Gift of the New Realm in Christ*, BTNT (Grand Rapids, MI: Zondervan Academic, 2021), 199.

6 David G. Peterson, *Commentary on Romans*, BTCP (Nashville: Holman Reference, 2017), 53.

kingdom of God" (14:17). And Paul finishes an account of his mission agenda with a quotation of Isaiah 11:1, where "the root of Jesse . . . arises to rule" (Rom. 15:12).[7]

The Background to Paul's Use of the Word "Gospel"

The word "gospel" or "good news," *euangelion*, is not unique to Paul or the New Testament. In the ancient world it was used to mean a message of good news in the political propaganda of the Roman Empire. For example, Josephus uses the word in his account of the "good news" of Vespasian becoming emperor in AD 69:

> When news spread in the east of the new emperor [Vespasian], every city celebrated the *good news* and offered sacrifices on his behalf. . . . On reaching Alexandria Vespasian was greeted by the *good news* from Rome and by embassies of congratulations from every part of the world, now his own, the whole empire being now secured and the Roman state saved beyond expectation.[a]

The political flavor of "gospel" as connoting a public announcement of universal significance prompting joyous celebration of a new era is not lost in Paul's usage. Indeed, Paul builds on the Old Testament prophets (in the Septuagint Greek translation), who use the term in the context of military victory. In Nahum 1:15 (2:1 LXX), the defeat of Assyria's king

7 Cf. Roy E. Ciampa, "Paul's Theology of the Gospel," in *Paul as Missionary: Identity, Activity, Theology, and Practice*, ed. Trevor J. Burke and Brian S. Rosner, LNTS 420 (Edinburgh: T&T Clark, 2011), 190: "According to Paul's theology of the gospel, God has acted and is acting through Christ's life, death, resurrection/exaltation and present reign as Lord over all creation to set all things right to the glory of his name."

is described as "good news." In Joel 2:32 (3:5 LXX), which Paul quotes in Romans 10:13, the prophet describes as "good news" the day when "everyone who calls on the name of the Lord will be saved." Most significantly for Paul, Isaiah uses the term in connection with the coming reign of God and the return from exile. As John Dickson has shown, "Paul's usage of gospel-terminology [esp. 'to preach the gospel'] was heavily influenced by . . . Isaiah 40:9, 52:7 and 61:1, wherein 'secular' messenger language had been transposed to a higher, eschatological level, depicting the end-time herald(s) commissioned by Israel's God to announce his salvific reign."[b] Paul quotes Isaiah 52:7 in Romans 10:15: "How beautiful are the feet of those who preach the good news [*tōn euangelizomenōn ta agatha*]!"

a Josephus, *The Jewish War*, LCL 3 (Cambridge, MA: Harvard University Press, 1928), 4.618, 656–57 (my translation based on the LCL Greek text).
b John P. Dickson, *Mission-Commitment in Ancient Judaism and in the Pauline Communities*, WUNT 2.159 (Tübingen: Mohr Siebeck, 2003), 176.

Romans as an Exposition of the Gospel

The theme of Romans is announced in 1:16–17: the gospel, which is attested by the Old Testament, is God's saving power in which the righteousness of God is revealed. The phrase "the righteousness of God" (*diskaiosynē theou*) is central to Paul's presentation of the gospel in the letter. It appears again in Romans 3:5, 21, 22; 10:3 (2x), along with "his [God's] righteousness" in 3:25, 26. Whether it refers to an activity of God, an attribute of God, or a status given to believers is debated. In terms of the usage of the phrase in the LXX, it is significant that God's righteousness and God's salvation often appear in poetic parallelism in Psalms and Isaiah (e.g., LXX Pss. 39:11; 50:16; 70:15; 97:2; 118:123; Isa. 33:6; 46:13; 51:5–6, 8; 62:1; 63:1). But more specifically, the LXX can speak of the eschatological revelation of God's righteousness and seems to be referring to God acting righteously to save his people. For example, Psalm 98:2 says,

> The Lord has made known his salvation;
> he has revealed his righteousness in the sight of the nations.
> (cf. Isa. 51:5–8)

Michael Bird combines activity and attribute, arguing that "God's righteousness is chiefly a way of designating his saving action as it is expressed in his feats of deliverance for his people. The righteousness of God then is the character of God embodied and enacted in his saving works."[8] On the other hand, the context of justification cautions against entirely ruling out the new righteous status of believers as at least part of the meaning of the phrase in Romans 3. Perhaps Stuhlmacher is right that Paul includes "both poles of the event of justification. . . . The gracious activity of God himself and the end result of the divine work in the form of the righteousness granted to the sinner."[9] We should allow that "the righteousness of God" can have different nuances depending on the context and not insist on a single definition. In Romans 1:17, its first occurrence in the letter, the expression is likely pregnant with meaning, delivering varied meanings in later contexts.

The words with the root *dik-* that appear in Romans include "righteousness" (*diskaiosynē*), "unrighteousness" (*adikia*), "unrighteous" (*adikos*), "righteous" (*dikaios*), "righteous decree" (*dikaiōma*), and the verb "justify" (*dikaioō*)—typically translated in English in a way that obscures the link to "righteousness."[10] These terms occur seventy-seven times in Romans compared to just sixty-nine times in Paul's other letters combined. *Gospel* and *righteousness* language are so central to the

8 Michel F. Bird, *The Saving Righteousness of God: Studies on Paul, Justification, and the New Perspective* (Milton Keynes, UK: Paternoster, 2006), 111.

9 P. Stuhlmacher, "The Theme of Romans," in *The Romans Debate*, rev. ed., ed. K. P. Donfried (Peabody, MA: Hendrickson, 1991), 339.

10 The translation "declare righteous" maintains the link to the other cognate terms.

argument and structure of Romans that it is helpful and appropriate to use them for an outline of the letter:

I. The gospel concerning God's Son (1:1–7)
II. Paul's desire to preach the gospel in Rome (1:8–15)
III. Theme: the righteousness of God revealed in the Gospel (1:16–17)
IV. God's righteousness in his wrath against sinners (1:18–3:20)
V. The saving righteousness of God: justification by faith (3:21–4:25)
VI. The effects of the righteousness of God: freedom and life in the Spirit: (5:1–8:39)
VII. The rejection of righteousness from God: the problem of Jewish unbelief (9:1–11:36)
VIII. God's righteousness in everyday life (12:1–15:13)
IX. The spread of the righteousness of God through Paul's mission (15:14–16:24)
X. Final summary of the gospel of the righteousness of God (16:25–27)

A brief survey of the main sections of Romans provides a good orientation to its contents:

Romans 1:18–4:25

In 1:18–3:20 Paul establishes the unrighteous condition of all human beings with the relentless drive of a trial lawyer. Both Jews and Gentiles are guilty before God and deserve his wrath. He also highlights the destructive behavior—of which the prophets and psalmists complain—that is addressed by God's transformation of individuals, societies, and the cosmos through the gospel as expounded in Romans 5–8. In 3:21–31 Paul announces that God has done what is needed for humanity to be declared righteous through the sacrificial death and resurrection of Jesus Christ. Our acceptance with God is neither by our own achievement nor dependent on keeping the law;

it is by faith. However, this is not contrary to the law but upholds the law (3:31), as Paul demonstrates in 4:1–25 with the examples of Abraham and David.

Romans 5:1–8:39

Paul explains that the new situation of the justified brings peace, hope, freedom, and life. Believers have a sure hope of final salvation, have been set free from the enslaving power of sin and the condemning power of the law, and are indwelt by the Holy Spirit who leads them to a life of righteousness.

Romans 9:1–11:36

Paul defends God against the charge of unrighteousness in the light of Israel's substantial failure to respond to the gospel and his consequent rejection of them. What of his pledge to Abraham and the patriarchs? Paul explains that, despite Israel's rejection of the righteousness of God by faith, God still remains faithful to his covenant promises.

Romans 12:1–15:13

Paul lays out the practical implications of the righteousness of God. In 12:1–13:14 believers are called to obedience and faith in their daily attitudes and actions. In the light of the coming consummation of salvation, they are to live in humility and love toward one another and in submission to civil authorities. In 14:1–15:13 Paul seeks to calm quarrels in the church by urging Jewish and Gentile believers to act responsibly toward one another in matters of social custom, acknowledging the lordship of Christ over their lives and following his example of sacrificial love.

Romans 15:14–16:27

Paul explains how he seeks to plant churches in unevangelized territories to fulfill his mission of extending the saving promises of God in the gospel to Gentiles. His final greetings to coworkers in the gospel demonstrate the interpersonal nature of this mission.

Biblical Theology and the Gospel in Romans

The logical flow of the argument of Romans, as presented above, is mirrored roughly in the sequence of the chapters of this book:

Chapters 2–3: The need for and provision of the righteousness of God
Chapter 4: The gospel of God's saving righteousness
Chapter 5: The human response to the gospel
Chapter 6: The witness of the Old Testament to the saving righteousness of God
Chapter 7: The person and work of Christ
Chapter 8: The benefits of the grace of God in the gospel
Chapter 9: The person and work of the Spirit
Chapter 10: Israel's rejection of the righteousness of God
Chapters 11–13: The implications of God's righteousness in everyday life
Chapter 14: The return of Christ and the end of all things

This book, however, is not merely an exposition of the big ideas of Romans as they appear in each of its main sections. Three considerations warn against thinking that these units of thought (Rom. 1:18–4:25; 5:1–8:39; 9:1–11:36; 12:1–15:13; 15:14–16:27) can be discussed in isolation from each other: (1) the cumulative nature of the argument of Romans; (2) the many topics associated with one unit of thought that are anticipated and/or taken further in others; and (3) the existence of many subthemes in Romans that are not the focus of any one section but, rather, span the entire letter.

A Cumulative Reading of Romans

Romans is the longest and most imposing of Paul's letters, with innumerable exegetical problems to solve and several libraries of long commentaries to negotiate. Therefore, we are tempted to read it in small chunks. However, such reading is unnatural for a letter like Romans. Rather than reading like a bowling ball, knocking over one text after another, we need to read Romans cumulatively like a snowball, seeing Paul's argument build with each text. Or, using a different analogy, if exegesis takes an atomistic approach, biblical theology is a molecular discipline, considering the place of each passage in the text as a whole.[11] In its first-century setting, Romans was likely read and listened to, in its entirety, in one sitting—giving readers and hearers the opportunity of "building up and establishing connections between different segments of the text."[12] Reading is a process of prospection and retrospection, where sentences act as indicators of something that is to come and later sentences take the minds of the readers back to earlier sentences.

Sometimes in Romans Paul introduces a point briefly and returns later to treat it at greater length. The way in which questions posed in Romans 3 are answered more fully later in the letter is a good example (see table 1.1).

Table 1.1 Prospective Questions in Romans 3

Question	Answer
Paul asks, "What advantage has the Jew? . . . What if some were unfaithful? Does their faithlessness nullify the faithfulness of God?" (Rom. 3:1–3)	Paul takes up the problem of Jewish unbelief and God's faithfulness in Rom. 9–11.
Paul asks, "Why not do evil that good may come?—as some people slanderously charge us with saying" (Rom. 3:8)	Paul addresses the objection that the gospel of God's grace leads to a license to sin in Rom. 6:1–23.
Paul asks, "Do we then overthrow the law by this faith?" (Rom. 3:31).	Paul defends the role of the law in full in Rom. 7–8.

Big Themes across the Letter

As noted above in the outline and survey of Romans, each major unit of the letter represents a step forward in the argument and focuses on key themes: universal sin, judgment, and salvation in Romans 1–4; hope, suffering, and life in Romans 5–8; and so on. However, while

11 This analogy was suggested to me by Graham Cole.

12 A. C. Thiselton, *New Horizons in Hermeneutics* (London: Marshall Pickering, 1992), 518.

such big themes are treated in depth in these units, there is further teaching across the letter on such topics.

The teaching of Romans on the subject of sin, for example, is not exhausted with the condemnation of all human beings in 1:18–3:20. In other parts of Romans we learn that sin entered the world through Adam's transgression (5:12), its effects stretch to the entire cosmos (8:19–22), and its future, final defeat is assured (16:20). While in Romans 1–3 human rebellion against God is described as "ungodliness" (1:18), "unrighteousness" (1:18, 29), "impurity" (1:24), "evil" (2:9), and "sin" (3:9, 20), these terms appear in other parts of the letter, along with "lawlessness" (6:19), "disobedience" (5:19), "trespass" (4:25; 5:15, 16, 17, 18; 11:11, 12), and "works of darkness" (13:12). In addition, there are other treatments of specific sins in many parts of the letter. In Romans 1 we see the sins of ignoring God, ingratitude, idolatry, and sexual immorality (1:18–28), as well as a lengthy vice list (1:29–32). Later in Romans, there are treatments of coveting (7:7–11) and judging fellow believers (14:1–15:7). Additional subjects in Romans 1–3 are also reinforced and developed in other parts of the letter, including the universal gospel invitation,[13] the death of Christ, the response of faith, the witness of the Old Testament, and the blessings of salvation.

Subthemes across the Letter

Various subthemes also appear across the letter. Although none of them is a main subject of a section, these subthemes are, nevertheless, also critical to a full presentation of the theology of Romans. These include, for example, slavery, obedience, glory, worship, resurrection, and suffering. Such topics provide color and texture to the letter's presentation of the gospel and its many implications. They also demonstrate the remarkable coherence of Paul's gospel theology in Romans.

Consider, for instance, the teaching of Romans on the mind and thinking.[14] The word "mind" (*nous*) first appears in 1:28, where Paul refers to the

13 See Rom. 2:5–11; 3:9, 22–23, 29–30; 4:9–12, 16–17; 9:24; 10:11–13; 11:32; 15:8–12.

14 See Craig S. Keener, *The Mind of the Spirit: Paul's Approach to Transformed Thinking* (Grand Rapids, MI: Baker Academic, 2016).

debased pagan mind. The *nous* then pops up five more times in the letter: 7:23, 25; 11:34; 12:2; and 14:5. However, this data does not exhaust the topic, as concepts are bigger than terms. To trace the theme of the mind across the letter we must take into account other words, such as the verbs "consider" (*logizomai*)[15] and "set one's mind on something" (*phroneō*).[16]

In brief, Romans

- describes and condemns the corrupted mind of the Gentile world (1:18–32);
- describes and condemns the knowledgeable mind of the Jewish world (7:7–25);
- condemns those who set their minds on the things of the flesh (8:5);
- commends a new way of thinking in Christ (6:1–11);
- prescribes a mind empowered by God's Spirit (8:5–7);
- commends being of the same mind toward one another in the body of Christ and not being haughty in mind (12:16; 15:5);[17] and
- urges a renewed mind in response to the gospel that is aligned with the values of the coming age (12:1–3).

The theme of the mind in Romans is impressively comprehensive, covering everything from the dynamics of Jewish and Gentile sin to a presentation of how the gospel transforms the behavior of those who belong to Christ. It even includes a humbling reminder that no one knows the mind (*nous*) of the Lord (Rom. 11:34, quoting Isa. 40:13)!

Conclusion

Biblical theology may be defined as "the theological interpretation of Scripture in and for the church. It proceeds with historical and literary sensitivity and seeks to analyze and synthesize the Bible's teaching about

15 Cf. e.g., Rom. 6:11: "*Consider* yourselves dead to sin and alive to Christ Jesus."

16 Cf. e.g., Rom. 8:5: "those who . . . *set their minds on* the things of the Spirit."

17 While most modern versions have a variation of "live in harmony with one another," NASB 1995 uses a more literal translation of *phroneō* ("to think") in these verses: "Be of the same mind toward one another" (12:16). May God "grant you to be of the same mind with one another" (15:5).

God and his relations to the world on its own terms, maintaining sight of the Bible's overarching narrative and Christocentric focus."[18] There is perhaps no book in the New Testament better suited to this task. The first step is to look at the need for the gospel in terms of universal human guilt before God (chapter 2) and universal human bondage to sin (chapter 3).

18 B. S. Rosner, "Biblical Theology," in *NDBT* 10.

2

Universal Human Guilt

All . . . are under sin.

ROMANS 3:9

IF THE GOSPEL IS "the power of God for salvation" (1:16), the first step in preaching it is to explain the predicament from which we need to be saved. Only when we plumb the depths of our desperate situation can we fully appreciate the scale and wonder of our rescue. Two phrases in Romans sum up the plight for which the gospel is the solution: All human beings are "under sin" (3:9) and "slaves of sin" (6:17, 20). Sin is both the guilt that condemns us and a power that enslaves us. The gospel meets universal human guilt and bondage with the good news of forgiveness and freedom.

Romans 1:18–3:20 is the longest explanation of the guilt of humanity before a righteous God in the whole Bible, and it is our primary focus in this chapter. "The theme of sin as an alien, potent and active power recurs in Romans 5–7,"[1] and this sobering and disturbing topic will be covered in chapter 3. In both cases, while sin and judgment are to the fore, there is much else to learn along the way. In 1:18–3:20, for example, there is implicit instruction on gospel

1 Cf. Leon L. Morris, "Sin, Guilt," in *DPL* 878.

living (see "Implicit Teaching on Christian Conduct in 1:18–3:20" below), a defense of the faithfulness of God (3:1–8), and teaching on the human constitution—our essence, limitations, and potential (see excursus below).

The dominant image in Romans 1:18–3:20 is a law court.[2] Much of the language and many themes in the unit have a legal flavor, including accountability, judgment, justice, excuses, charges, and condemnation. In addition, the frequent use of the style of diatribe—a dialogical form of expression engaging imaginary opponents—adds to the impression of a court case with defendants and a prosecutor. Paul addresses such opponents (2:1–4, 17–24) and answers their objections (2:25–29; 3:3–4, 9, 19–20). The big ideas of the unit are the impartiality of the judgment of God and universal human culpability.

The argument of 1:18–3:20, which will inform the outline of this chapter, fits remarkably well with the lawcourt metaphor:

- I. Summary indictment (1:18)
    - A. First defendant: Gentiles (1:19–32)
        1. Idolatry (1:19–23, 25)
        2. Dishonorable passions (1:24, 26–27)
        3. Debased minds (1:28–32)
    - B. Second defendant: Jews (2:1–5, 17–29)
        1. Self-righteousness and presumption (2:1–5)
        2. Pride and hypocrisy (2:17–29)
- II. The standards of God's judgment (2:6–16)
- III. The objection of Jewish exceptionalism (3:1–8)
- IV. Closing statement (3:9–20)
    - A. The summary charge (3:9)
    - B. Scriptural evidence (3:10–18)
    - C. The verdict (3:19–20)

2 Cf. N. T. Wright, "The Letter to the Romans," in *NIB* 10:457, commenting on 3:9: "Paul now begins a lawcourt metaphor, which he will develop further in vv. 19–20. He has already laid a charge, like a plaintiff in a case. . . . By 'already charged' he is referring back, obviously, to the argument that began in 1:18."

The metaphor of the law court continues until the end of Romans 4 with a surprise acquittal announced in 3:21–31 and appeal to two scriptural legal precedents (Abraham and David) for being declared righteous by faith and not works presented in 4:1–25.

Summary Indictment (1:18)

The first step in Paul's exposition of the gospel in Romans is to announce God's wrath in response to human sin. In the rest of Romans 1, this wrath is described as God "handing people over" (*paradidōmi*; ESV: "gave them up") to the consequences of their sin in the present (1:24, 26, 28). In the rest of Romans, God's wrath refers to his righteous anger on the coming day of judgment (2:5, 8; 3:5; 4:15; 5:9; 9:22; 12:19). "God's wrath is no capricious emotion but the necessary response of a perfect and holy God to violations of his will."[3] How palatable we find the doctrine of God's wrath will depend on our experience and awareness of the "ruin and misery" (3:16) of human evil.

There is, however, some good news on the matter of God handing people over to sin's consequences. Another two instances of *paradidōmi* in Romans point to God acting to save those under his wrath: The gospel proclaims that God handed Jesus over for our trespasses (4:25) and handed Jesus over to death for us all (8:32), thereby paying the price of our justification and forgiveness.

First Defendant: Gentiles (1:19–32)

Gentiles are under God's wrath because they have rejected the knowledge of God available to them and indulged in unrighteousness. In Romans 1 Paul underscores repeatedly that they deserve their condemnation. Since they suppress the truth about God that he showed them and made plain to them—his existence and power visible in the creation—they are "without excuse" (1:20). Paul highlights idolatry and sexual immorality as their most egregious sins.

3 Douglas J. Moo, *Encountering the Book of Romans: A Theological Survey*, 2nd ed. (Grand Rapids, MI: Baker Academic, 2014), 38.

IDOLATRY (1:19–23, 25)

The chief sin of the Gentiles is their exchanging of "the glory of the immortal God for images" (1:23). As Michael Gorman writes, "When we abandon and dismiss God, someone or something happily moves in and becomes our god."[4] There is no better proof of foolish thinking and foolish hearts (1:21) than the sin of idolatry. The Bible critiques idolatry in four complementary ways, each of which underscores its foolishness: idolatry (1) frustrates, (2) contaminates, and (3) degrades its worshippers, who (4) eventually incur the jealous judgment of God. These four effects are the reverse of what the true and living God does for those who trust in him (things we see in the rest of Romans): the true and living God saves, purifies, transforms, and justifies believers in Christ.[5]

All people know enough about God to understand that they should honor and give thanks to him. But their wicked abuse of God and other people (see 1:28–32) merits his judgment. "It is a predicament that leads to death (1:32; cf. 6:23a)—both a sort of living death now and an eternal death to come."[6]

DISHONORABLE PASSIONS (1:24, 26–27)

If the primary reason for God's wrath against Gentiles is their idolatry, the result of his wrath is that they are given over to perverted sexual practices and a depraved mind. The "shameful lusts" (1:26 NIV) Paul highlights refer to the exchanging of natural for unnatural sex (1:24, 26–27), an idiom meaning "contrary to the pattern of male and female relations described in Gen. 1."[7] Many attempts have been made to avoid reading these verses as disapproval of all homosexual

4 Michael J. Gorman, *Romans: A Theological and Pastoral Commentary* (Grand Rapids, MI: Eerdmans, 2022), 83.

5 See Brian S. Rosner, "Idolatry," in *Dictionary of Scripture and Ethics*, ed. Joel Green, Jacqueline Lapsley, Rebekah Miles, and Allen Verhey (Grand Rapids, MI: Baker Academic, 2011), 392–94.

6 Gorman, *Romans*, 89.

7 Gorman, *Romans*, 85. Paul uses the same Greek words for male and female that appear in LXX Gen. 1:27. Cf. G. J. Wenham, "The Old Testament Attitude to Homosexuality,"

relations.[8] That these have proven to be unsuccessful is seen in the fact that many scholars who approve of homosexual practices still regard the passage as "a completely unambiguous condemnation of all homosexual activity."[9]

That Paul did not regard homosexual relations as an especially heinous sin, a peak form of evil, is clear from the vice list in 1 Corinthians 6:9–10 where it sits alongside other forms of sexual immorality, drunkenness, reviling, and greed. The focus on the sin of homosexual relations (Rom. 1:24, 26–27) may in part be explained by two things it shares with the sin of idolatry: (1) Both consist of a failure to respond appropriately to the created order. (2) Both involve a tragic exchange. Whereas idolatry exchanges (*allassō*) the glory of God for images (1:23) and exchanges (*metallassō*) "the truth about God for a lie" (1:25), homosexual practice exchanges (*metallassō*) "natural relations for those that are contrary to nature" (1:26).

DEBASED MINDS (1:28–32)

The downward spiral of sin continues with a second devastating consequence of idolatry—namely, being given over to "a debased mind" (1:28; cf. futile thinking in 1:21) and, as a result, "filled with all manner of unrighteousness" (1:29). In 1:29–31 Paul lists twenty ugly sins that lead to moral chaos and do inestimable harm to individuals, families, and whole societies. The last five items (1:30–31) begin with the Greek letter alpha and, thereby, pack a climactic rhetorical punch. To retain the assonance in English, using a similar sounding suffix, we might translate that those who do not see fit to acknowledge God are "rebellious, senseless, faithless, heartless, ruthless." The dire depiction of humanity in rebellion against God in Romans 1 is capped off with people not only doing heartless and

---

ExpTim 102, no. 9 (1990–91): 359–63, who convincingly traces the Old Testament opposition to homosexuality to Israel's doctrine of creation in Gen. 1–3.

8 Gorman, *Romans*, 86, lists eleven such explanations, such as Paul only condemns casual, exploitative, cultic, or excessively lustful homosexual relations.

9 E. P. Sanders, *Paul: The Apostle's Life, Letters, and Thought* (Minneapolis: Fortress, 2015), 373.

ruthless things, "but even applaud[ing] others who practice them" (1:32 NRSV).

Second Defendant: Jews (2:1–5, 17–29)

In Romans 2:1–5 and 2:17–29, Paul turns his attention to those who would pass judgment on the Gentiles described in 1:19–32. While some have suggested that Paul is initially addressing people with high moral standards, whether Jews or Gentiles, there are good reasons to think that he is addressing Jews (even though he does not specifically mention Jews until 2:17). As Thomas Schreiner points out, Jews criticized Gentiles for the sorts of behavior described in 1:19–32. "The attitude expressed in 2:3–4 fits Jews who plead their covenant relationship" as exempting them from God's judgment, and "the primary thrust of verses 12–16 is that the Jews have no [salvific] advantage despite having the law."[10]

SELF-RIGHTEOUSNESS AND PRESUMPTION (2:1–5)

In 2:1 Paul reveals the conclusion to which he is heading in 3:20: Jews, no less than Gentiles, are "under sin" (3:9) and "have no excuse" (2:1; cf. 1:20). Jews who think of themselves as morally superior to Gentiles are condemned for committing many of the same sins—perhaps not idolatry and sexual immorality but certainly some of the behaviors listed in 1:29–31 such as pride and boasting. Paul makes clear that being the covenant people of God does not exempt Jews from the judgment of God (2:2–5).

PRIDE AND HYPOCRISY (2:17–29)

In 2:17–20 (cf. 9:4–5) Paul lists the advantages of being a Jew, highlighting especially their possession of the law of Moses (see 2:17, 20). He then goes on to insist that such benefits fall short of bringing salvation. The mere possession of the law does not guarantee God's favor. The law was given to be obeyed, and breaking it provokes the wrath of God.

10 Thomas R. Schreiner, *Romans*, 2nd ed., BECNT (Grand Rapids, MI: Baker Academic, 2018), 112.

Paul charges that the Jews do not practice what they preach (2:21–22). Far from being superior to the Gentiles, the Jews malign the reputation of God among the Gentiles because of their disobedience (Rom. 2:23–24; cf. Isa. 52:5). Circumcision, the mark of their membership in the people of God, will also not exempt Jews from judgment (Rom. 2:25–29). This whole section is a sobering reminder that religious affiliation and externals must never become the things in which we trust for our standing before God. A righteous standing before God is by grace alone through faith alone.

The Standards of God's Judgment (2:6–16)

Paul interrupts his interrogation of Jewish defendants to review the basis on which God will "judge the world" (Rom. 3:6). A human court is only as good as its underlying principles and its adherence to the rule of law. With this in mind, the thoroughness and equity of God's standards of judgment as laid out in Romans 2:6–16 is reassuring. We can be fully confident that the judge of all the earth will do what is just (Gen. 18:25). "The judgment of God" (Rom. 2:3) will be

- according to truth (2:2),
- according to works (2:6),
- impartial (2:11),
- according to a person's response to the available light of law and conscience (2:12, 15),
- an uncovering of what people have kept secret (2:16), and
- exercised through Jesus Christ (2:16).

In 2:6–16 Paul defends the perfect justice of God by insisting that he will give to people what they are due. This passage raises a tension in Paul's argument: "The doers of the law who will be justified" (2:13) seems to contradict "by works of the law no human being will be justified" (3:20). Two solutions to this problem are worth considering. First, Paul is laying out the conditions that a person must meet ("persistence in doing good," 2:7 NIV) to be given eternal life, but as

3:10–18 makes clear, no one meets those conditions. Second, "in 2:7 and 10 Paul is speaking of Christians who keep the law by the power of the Holy Spirit."[11]

In favor of the second view, 2:13 can be read in light of 2:14–16 and 2:25–27 where Gentile Christians do the law out of faith. Paul is clear throughout Romans that justification is by faith (see chapter 5 below), and he distinguishes between believing and working when it comes to a right standing with God (Rom. 4:4–5; cf. Gal. 3:1–5). Works righteousness is excluded (Rom. 3:19–20, 27–31; 9:30–33). God works in us so that his verdict at the final judgment is in accord with his work in us now by his Spirit (Rom. 8:1–17). As Schreiner notes, "Paul elsewhere teaches that works are necessary to enter the kingdom of God (cf. 1 Cor. 6:9–11; 2 Cor. 5:10)."[12] As it turns out, Paul uses *dia* ("through") and *ek* ("by/from") to indicate that faith is the instrument through which people are justified (Rom. 3:22, 25; 5:1; Gal. 2:16) and uses *kata* ("according to / in accordance with") when it comes to the role of works at the final judgment: "He will render to each one according to his works" (Rom. 2:6; cf. "whose end will be according to their deeds," 2 Cor. 11:15 NASB 1995). Justification is by grace through faith, and this verdict leads to and is congruent with a life of obedience. In the context of Romans 1–3, this unit contributes both to Paul's defense of God's impartiality and justice and to the transformative impact of the gospel.

Another question is raised by 2:12–16 that is vital to Paul's argument that "all, both Jews and Greeks, are under sin" (3:9): What role does the law play in the condemnation of Gentiles? At first blush, the answer would seem to be that the law has no role to play: Gentiles "have sinned without the law" (2:12) and "do not have the law" (2:14). However, the passage also affirms that Gentiles sometimes "by nature do what the law requires" (2:14), showing that "the work of the law is written on their hearts" (2:15). As Bryan Blazosky contends, "The degree to which νόμος [the law] functions as a criterion for judgment differs between

11 Schreiner, *Romans*, 124.
12 Schreiner, *Romans*, 124.

Jews and Gentiles (2:12); but νόμος will nevertheless stand as a witness, alongside conscience, condemning both Jew and Gentile for failure to keep its righteous requirements."[13] Romans 2:12–16 contributes to Paul's insistence on God's impartiality at the final judgment by explaining that "both Jew (those 'in the law') and Gentile (those 'apart from the law') will be impartially judged according to the standard of whether or not they have *done* the law."[14]

The Objection of Jewish Exceptionalism (3:1–8)

"Romans 3:1–8 is one of the most difficult texts in the whole letter,"[15] in part because in addressing the question of God's faithfulness to his covenant people—"What advantage has the Jew?" (3:1)—Paul only gives a partial answer. We must wait until Romans 9–11 for his full reply (see chapter 10 below). Here Paul imagines a Jew asking whether there is any benefit in being a Jew if they are under the same verdict of condemnation as Gentiles. And if the Jews are under sin, does God remain faithful to his promises? The issue goes to the heart of the character of God—specifically, whether he is faithful (3:3) and righteous (3:5). Can God be trusted to keep his promises and do what is right? Defending the character of God in light of the revelation of his righteousness in the gospel, especially in his dealings with Israel his chosen people, is a major theme in Romans.

Paul's short reply in 3:1–8 affirms Jewish identity as valuable (3:2; cf. 9:4–5) but insists that "God's righteous judgment is an expression of his faithfulness."[16] God's righteousness is both a judging and a saving righteousness. Paul affirms that God continues to be faithful to his covenant people, for "the gifts and the calling of God are irrevocable"

13 Bryan Blazosky, *The Law's Universal Condemning and Enslaving Power: Reading Paul, the Old Testament, and Second Temple Jewish Literature* (University Park, PA: Eisenbrauns, 2019), 150.

14 A. A. Das, *Paul, the Law, and the Covenant* (Peabody, MA: Hendrickson, 2001), 179 (emphasis in original).

15 Schreiner, *Romans*, 155.

16 David G. Peterson, *Commentary on Romans*, BTCP (Nashville: Holman Reference, 2017), 168.

(11:29). However, God's faithfulness does not exempt Jews from judgment. After all, the covenant with Israel includes both promises of blessing for obedience and cursing for disobedience.

Closing Statement (3:9–20)

"What then" (3:9) do we conclude at the end of Paul's lengthy series of indictments against "all [the] ungodliness and unrighteousness of men" (1:18)? Paul sums up his lengthy case against all human beings, both Jews and Gentiles, with a devastating charge supported by scriptural proof (3:9–18): We all stand under sin. Indeed, the whole world stands condemned before God (3:19–20).

The Summary Charge (3:9)

Paul sums up his argument from 1:18–3:8 by declaring that he has "already reached a charge of guilt" (*proaitiaomai*)[17] on "both Jews and Greeks [i.e., Gentiles]"—namely, that all people "are under sin" (3:9). The elliptical phrase "under sin" is regularly understood in commentaries and some translations as "under the power of sin" (e.g., NIV, NRSV). However, while Romans teaches that sin reigns, enslaves, rules, and exercises lordship (see chapter 3 on Rom. 5–7), that is not Paul's point in 3:9. Sin as guilt deserving God's righteous condemnation, and wrath is the sustained focus of Romans 1–3. The immediately preceding context supports this, with 3:7 and 3:8 having the just condemnation of sinners in view, a point driven home in 3:19 with "the whole world" being "held accountable to God." The Greek terms, "already reaching a charge of guilt" (*proaitiaomai*) in 3:9 and "holding someone to account" (*hupodikos*) in 3:19 have forensic connotations. The phrase "under sin" does require interpretation, but Paul's meaning in the context of Romans 1–3 is clearly "under the condemnation / guilt of sin." The thrust of 3:9–20 is well captured by the heading in the CSB: "The Whole World Guilty before God."[18]

17 Cf. "Προαιτιάομαι," in BDAG 865.

18 Cf. REB, NASB 1995, and the German Hoffnung für Alle, which have similar headings.

Scriptural Evidence (3:10–18)

The bulk of Paul's closing statement is a series of quotations from the Old Testament (Pss. 13:2–3, 5; 5:10; 9:2–8; 35:2; 139:4; Isa. 59:7–8; cf. Eccl. 7:20) to support the verdict of universal human sinfulness deserving condemnation. This impressive catena of texts is particularly relevant to the Jews who saw themselves as having been "entrusted with the oracles of God" (Rom. 3:2; cf. 2:17–20).[19] The Jews have been Paul's focus since 2:1, and he has taken great pains to establish their guilt and culpability along with Gentiles while at the same time defending God's faithfulness and righteousness.

In 3:10–12 the universality of sin is brutally underscored: "None," "not one," "no one" (3x), "not even one" "is righteous," "understands," "seeks for God," or "does good." Specific charges are laid in 3:13–17. First, Paul lists sins of wicked speech, such as "curses and bitterness," using a graphic figure of speech: "Their throat is an open grave" (3:13–14). Then, 3:15–17 describes the "ruin and misery" (3:16) that sin inflicts on human society. Finally, the root cause of such evil is identified: People have "no fear of God" to restrain them from evil (3:18). Paul's selection of Old Testament texts mentions many body parts—throats, tongues, lips, mouths, feet, and eyes—leaving an impression of the spread of sin to every part of human conduct. It is not that all human beings behave in all these ways all the time. But all of us are capable of such evil conduct, and each of us has besetting sins. Human beings are "inventors of evil" (1:30). More and worse forms of wickedness are possible and propagated beyond the twenty items in 1:29–31. Human evil is the original diverse and inclusive industry.

The Verdict (3:19–20)

Paul's final summation is that the whole world, both Jews and Gentiles, is accountable to God and guilty as charged. The law will shut every mouth and condemn every sinner. Clearly Jews are condemned as those

19 Cf. Douglas J. Moo, *A Theology of Paul and His Letters: The Gift of the New Realm in Christ*, BTNT (Grand Rapids, MI: Zondervan Academic, 2021), 208: "What these texts say has special application to Jews."

"under the law" (3:19).[20] What about Gentiles? While commentators debate the logic of 3:19, in the light of 2:12–16 (see above) it is best to understand Gentiles as included in those who are in "the realm of the law [*en tō nomō*]" (3:19 my translation) "in that they are fully aware of the moral norms stated in the law."[21] The scriptural evidence cited in 3:10–18 supports this conclusion (see above). Whereas the five Davidic psalms Paul cites condemn fools and David's Gentile enemies, the Isaiah citation speaks against Israel. "Paul uses the unified voices of Israel's greatest king and prophet to affirm the equality of humanity's plight"[22] under the condemnation of sin.

Implicit Teaching on Christian Conduct in 1:18–3:20

While the primary purpose of Romans 1–3 is to establish the verdict that all human beings lack righteousness and deserve God's wrath, it is a mistake to limit it to this function alone. The keen relevance of the passage to Christians should not be missed. The unit has at least two additional functions: (1) It magnifies the grace of God in the gospel by portraying in lurid detail the depths of human depravity; (2) it serves as moral teaching for all Christians. As Titus 2:11–12 states, "The grace of God has appeared, bringing salvation for all people, training us to renounce ungodliness and worldly passions, and to live self-controlled, upright, and godly lives in the present age." Paul's goal of transforming the lives of those who trust in Christ is not left until the second half of the letter. Romans 1–3 presents an inventory of sins to avoid and a lifestyle that is not in keeping with the new identity of those who have died and been raised with Christ.

Reading Romans 1–3, believers are reminded that they are to say no to unrighteousness (1:18, 29; 2:8; 3:5, 10), evil/wickedness (1:30; 2:9; 3:8), pride and arrogance (2:1–5, 17, 21), sexual immorality (1:26–28; 2:22), idolatry (1:25; 2:22), violence (1:29–30; 3:15), evil speech (1:29;

20 "All who have sinned under the law [i.e., Jews] will be judged by the law" (2:12; cf. 2:23).

21 Thomas R. Schreiner, *40 Questions about Christians and the Biblical Law* (Grand Rapids, MI: Kregel, 2010), 79.

22 Blazosky, *The Law's Universal Condemning and Enslaving Power*, 153.

3:7, 13–15), blasphemy (1:30; 2:24; 3:8), unfaithfulness (1:31; 3:3), and strife (1:29; 2:8). By implication, they are to exult in God's glory (1:21, 23, 30; 2:23; 3:11, 18) and affirm the truth about God (1:18, 25; 2:8; 3:4).[23]

Much of the moral teaching in the rest of Romans presents the alternative to such behavior. For example, along with the encouragement to renounce pride (11:18, 20, 25; 14:4, 10), the positive alternative of humility is promoted: "Think [about yourself] with sober judgment" (12:3), "outdo one another in showing honor" (12:10), and "do not be haughty, but associate with the lowly" (12:16). And if those who reject God do not know "the way of peace" (3:17), believers are to "live in harmony with one another" (12:16) and "live peaceably with all" (12:18). The whole of Romans contributes to Paul's moral vision of gospel living.

The Anthropological Terms in Romans[a]

The Bible's so-called anthropological terms, words that describe what constitutes a human being, reveal something about our essence, limitations, and potential. They appear across Romans, with no less than seven such terms in Romans 1–2 alone: *body* (1:24), *flesh* (2:28; 3:20), *heart* (1:21, 24; 2:5, 15, 29), *mind* (1:28), *soul* (2:9), *spirit* (2:29), and *conscience* (2:15). In this brief digression, I consider six of the most important.[b] In line with the Old Testament's anthropology, these are best understood as aspects of a human being rather than parts of a human being. In other words, they represent human existence viewed from different angles. The six terms can be considered in pairs: *body* and *flesh*, *mind* and *heart*, *soul* and *spirit*.

23 Cf. the table in Michael F. Bird, *Romans*, SGBC 6 (Grand Rapids, MI: Zondervan Academic, 2016), 99.

Paul uses the term *sōma* to describe the "body." It is not so much that we have a body but that we are embodied. When Paul writes to the Christians in Rome, "Present your bodies as a living sacrifice" (12:1), he is telling them to offer their whole being not just part of their existence. The parallel in 6:13 makes this clear when he exhorts them to "present yourselves to God." Paul sees us as embodied and therefore social beings, defined in part by our social interdependence and responsibility.

In Paul's letters, "flesh," *sarx*, is a related term that overlaps with "body." It has a wide range of meanings and is variously translated. For example, in Romans, the NIV renders *sarx* as "earthly life" (1:3), "physical" (2:28), "one" (as in "no one," 3:20), "flesh" (e.g., 4:1; 7:5; 8:3–9), "human limitations" (6:19), "sinful nature" (7:18), "[my] own race" (9:3), and "human [ancestry]" (9:5). The spectrum of meaning of "flesh" runs from human needs, through human weakness and desires, through human imperfection and corruption, to human sin and rebellion against God. Like Paul's use of *sōma*, *sarx* denotes the whole person but from the point of view of our frailty, weakness, and vulnerability to destructive desires. The main difference is that, whereas for the most part *sōma* is morally neutral, in many cases *sarx* is morally negative.

For Paul the "mind," *nous*, is the perceiving, thinking, determining, rational "I." We are rational beings, capable of soaring to the heights of reflective thought. The transformation of our behavior comes via a renewing of our minds so that we affirm that God's will is thoroughly wholesome and good (12:2).

The "heart," *kardia*, on the other hand, is the seat of human emotions and will. It overlaps with the mind in that some of the usage locates thought in the heart as well. The heart as the center of emotions is evident in texts such as 5:5, where "God's love has been poured out into our hearts." As a generalization, the mind is associated with the rational "I" and the heart with the emotional "I." But there is a fair degree of overlap. That human beings are both thinking and feeling beings is clear.

Greek *psychē*, "soul," in Paul's letters regularly refers to the whole person. We are living beings, animated by the mystery of life as a gift. It does not refer to a part of a person but is simply one way of describing human beings: "Let every person [*pasa psychē*, "every soul"] be subject to the governing authorities" (13:1). "Greet Prisca and Aquila, my fellow workers in Christ Jesus, who risked their necks for my life [*hyper tēs psychēs mou*, "for my soul"]" (16:3–4).

When it comes to *pneuma*, "spirit," what or whom Paul is referring to in his letters is not always clear. There are around twenty cases where the referent is clearly the human spirit and well over one hundred where the Spirit of God is in view. Apparently, the human spirit and the Spirit of God are closely related. The human spirit is that aspect of the human person that relates directly to God. Paul writes, "I serve [God] with my spirit" (1:9). Correspondingly, when he conceives of God as relating to us he can say that "the Spirit [of God] himself bears witness with our spirit" (8:16). For Paul, "spirit" denotes the Godward dimension of our existence, and the "soul" is connected to our life itself and its vitality. From our *psychē* we know that we are alive; from our *pneuma* we know that we can be alive to God.

What is a human being? We are embodied beings, *sōma*, and are therefore social, defined in part by social interdependence and responsibility. We are also fleshly, *sarx*—that is, frail and weak beings, conditioned by the inevitability of our death and driven by our desires, many of which are sinful. We are rational beings, *nous*, capable of soaring to the heights of reflective thought. And we are also experiencing beings with a heart, *kardia*, capable of emotions, thought, and will. We are living beings, *psychē*, animated by the mystery of life as a gift and also spiritual beings, *pneuma*, with the capacity to relate directly to God.

a This excursus is a summary of Brian S. Rosner, *Known by God: A Biblical Theology of Personal Identity*, BTFL (Grand Rapids, MI: Zondervan Academic, 2017), 67–74. Used by permission.

b The following discussion builds on the summary of Paul's anthropology in James D. G. Dunn, *The Theology of Paul the Apostle* (Edinburgh: T&T Clark, 1998), 51–78.

Conclusion

Romans 1–3 lays out the case that all human beings, both Jews and Gentiles, are under sin and deserve God's wrath. The next chapter completes the picture of humanity's perilous plight to which the gospel is the solution. In Romans 5–7 we move from the image of the lawcourt to one of a slave market, from being "under sin" to being "enslaved to sin."

3

Universal Human Bondage

Slaves of sin.

ROMANS 6:17, 20

IF PAUL PORTRAYS the singular plight of Jews and Gentiles in Romans 1–3, focusing on sin as guilt, he adds to the picture in Romans 5–8 by rehearsing the plight of all believers in Christ and focusing on sin as a power. Of course, Romans 5–8 covers much more than the topic of sin as a power. Elsewhere in this book, we look at what the section contributes to the teaching of Romans on salvation (chapter 4), responding to the gospel (chapter 5), the work of Christ (chapter 7), the work of the Spirit (chapter 9), the Christian life (chapter 11), and the end of all things (chapter 14). But the foundation of all of this vital teaching is the grim diagnosis that human beings are slaves of sin. Only when we face this dark and disturbing doctrine can we appreciate the deliverance and freedom that the gospel brings.[1] The subject of sin as an enslaving power, perhaps like no other, also

1 Cf. Beverley Gaventa, "The Cosmic Power of Sin in Paul's Letter to the Romans," *Int* 58, no. 3 (2024): 229, observes, "Paul's letter to the Romans depicts Sin as one of the anti-God powers whose final defeat the death and resurrection of Jesus Christ guarantees. The framework of cosmic battle is essential for reading and interpreting this letter in the life of the church."

emphasizes the need for the power of God in the gospel and the ongoing strengthening that believers need.

The Personification of Sin

The word "sin," *hamartia,* occurs forty-eight times in Romans with a concentration of forty-two occurrences in 5:12–8:17.[2] The vast majority of these are in the singular, with just three in the plural (two of which are in Old Testament quotations). This data, combined with "sin" as the subject of many active verbs, suggests that in Romans 5–8 sin has "quasi-personal powers."[3] Beverley Gaventa writes,

> Paul does not confine his comments about sin to human behavior, to sin as misdeeds, omitted deeds, even to perverted thoughts and plans. Instead, in Romans in particular, sin is Sin—not a lower-case transgression, not even a human disposition or flaw in human nature, but an upper-case Power that enslaves humankind and stands over against God.[4]

Indeed, in the drama of salvation in Romans 5–8, sin is a major character: Sin came into the world (5:12), increased trespasses (5:20), seized an opportunity and produced all kinds of covetousness (7:8), came alive and killed Paul (7:9), brought about death (7:13), and dwells within Paul (7:17). Sin exercises dominion over human beings (5:21; 6:12, 14) and acts as slave master over them (6:17; 7:25). Its power is exercised not just over individuals but also over communities (6:6, 16–20); even the entire creation needs to be set free from sin's power (8:21). Salvation involves being liberated from sin (6:14) and death (6:9). In Romans 5–8, being rescued from sin, death, and the flesh (and Satan in 16:20) is an integral part of the good news of the gospel. The extent to which Paul considers sin a cosmic tyrant in some literal sense, a view that fits well

2 "Sin" only appears sixteen times in the rest of Paul's letters.

3 Douglas J. Moo, *A Theology of Paul and His Letters: The Gift of the New Realm in Christ,* BTNT (Grand Rapids, MI: Zondervan Academic, 2021), 410.

4 Gaventa, "The Cosmic Power of Sin," 231.

with the apocalyptic view of Paul's theology,[5] is a subject of ongoing scholarly debate.

Viewing the atonement as penal substitution to save from the guilt of sin and viewing the atonement as victory over the power of sin should not be pitted against each other as rival presentations of salvation. Paul clearly affirms both. While Romans 5–8 focuses on victory over sin as a power, the beginning and end of the unit restate the truth of justification by faith (5:1; 8:1, 33–34), which focuses on sin as guilt. Moreover, the theme of the letter—the saving righteousness of God—not only applies to sin as guilt but also applies to our need for righteousness to liberate from sin's dominion: "When you were slaves of sin, you were free in regard to righteousness" (6:20).

Sin as a Power in Romans 5–8

The unit is held together by a repeated formula that provides the solution to the tyrannical power of sin: We are saved "through" or "in" our Lord Jesus Christ (5:1, 11; 6:23; 7:25; 8:39). The four chapters address different dimensions of sin's power over human beings and our deliverance through union with Christ in his death and resurrection:

- Believers have peace with God and the sure hope of final salvation based on God's love and grace, which have brought about a righteousness-life solidarity in Christ that is just as universal but far superior to the sin-death solidarity in Adam (5:1–21).
- Believers are set free from sin as a power through union with Christ and are enslaved to God, resulting in progress in holiness that leads to eternal life (6:1–23).
- Believers are set free from the law through the death of Christ, but the law remains holy and good, exposing sin that inevitably brings death (7:1–25).

5 Cf. Moo, *Theology*, 410: "We must be careful to recognize just what Paul is trying to claim by speaking of sin in this way—especially critical is the need to allow room for metaphor and rhetoric."

- Believers have the life-giving Holy Spirit who has freed them from the power of sin and death and who leads them onward in a life of righteousness until final salvation, guaranteed by the plan and character of God (8:1–39).

We will return to each of these passages in later chapters of this book when considering other dimensions of the gospel. For now, it is important to note that sin does not act alone in enslaving humanity. In 5:12–8:17 sin has three partners in making slaves of human beings: the law,[6] death, and the flesh. Blazosky offers a helpful summary: "Through the repeated themes of slavery and death, Paul unites the powers of darkness together, resulting in a unified presentation of the human predicament. It is not possible for [sin] to reign apart from the [law], nor is it possible for [sin], the [law], and [death] to enslave apart from flesh."[7] Indeed, 7:4–6 and 8:2–8 make clear that being "in the flesh" (*en sarki*) enables sin, death, and the law to enslave people.

As Blazosky points out, the work of Christ and the Spirit brings deliverance from this terrible captivity:

> The answer to [death] is the [death] of Jesus (5:15–21; 6:9; 7:24) and the power of the life-giving Spirit (8:2). The answer to [sin] is Jesus's death as a sin offering (8:3), our union in that death (5:20–21; 6:2–10; 8:3) and the liberating work of the life-giving Spirit (8:2). . . . Likewise, freedom from the [law] comes through the body of Christ and the work of the Spirit (7:4–6; cf. 8:2–3), and freedom from the [flesh] comes through the [flesh] of God's Son and the strength of the indwelling Spirit (7:5–6; 8:2–13). In 5:12–8:17, all believers were

6 The law plays a pivotal role in both the guilt and power of sin, with *nomos* occurring twenty-three times in Rom. 1–3 and thirty-three times in Rom. 5–8 (with just eighteen occurrences in the rest of the letter).

7 Bryan Blazosky, *The Law's Universal Condemning and Enslaving Power: Reading Paul, the Old Testament, and Second Temple Jewish Literature* (University Park, PA: Eisenbrauns, 2019), 162. I have replaced the few Greek words in this quotation with English words in brackets.

> formerly [in the flesh] and subject to the alliance of sin, the law, and death; but now, every believer is [in the Spirit, in Christ], and freed from every enslaving power.[8]

Paul's use of two verbs in Romans 5–7 meaning "reign" and "rule over"—*basileuō* and *kurieuō*—underscore both the enslaving power of sin and our liberation in Christ:

- Death *reigned* from Adam to Moses because of Adam's trespass (5:14).
- Death *reigns* through Adam's trespass, and those who receive the gracious gift of righteousness *reign* in life through Jesus Christ (5:17).
- If sin *reigns* in death, grace *reigns* through righteousness (5:21).
- Believers are not to let sin *reign* in their mortal bodies (6:12).
- Since Christ has been raised from the dead, death no longer *rules* over him (6:9).
- Sin will no longer *rule* over believers because we are no longer under the law but under grace (6:14).
- Having died with Christ, the law no longer *rules* over believers in Christ, and those who receive the gift of righteousness *reign* in life through Jesus Christ (7:1).

Sin's power affects not only individuals but also the societies and communities in which we live. We are condemned to live in a world full of violence, oppression, injustice, danger, and so on—all of which is evidence of the power and reign of sin. We are surrounded by every kind of wickedness (cf. 1:18–32; 3:10–18). Enslavement to sin goes well beyond our individual failings.

Sin as a power in Romans 5–8 raises two issues of critical importance for the theology of Romans: (1) the role of narrative in the theology of

8 Blazosky, *The Law's Universal Condemning and Enslaving Power*, 161–62. I have replaced the few Greek words in this quotation with English words in brackets. For more on the work of Christ and the Spirit, see chaps. 7 and 9 below, respectively.

Romans in light of the focus on the story of Adam's trespass and its consequences; (2) the question of individual and corporate identity given the focus on Adam and Christ as representatives of other human beings.

Underlying Stories in Romans

A recent area of research on Paul focuses on the role of narrative in his theology.[9] Whether we call this new discipline the narrative dynamics, narrative theology, or narratival substructures of Paul's letters, there is no doubt that stories underlie much of Paul's teaching. The gospel, "promised [by God] beforehand through his prophets in the holy Scriptures" (1:2), is the story of Jesus Christ (1:3–4). In fact, Romans presents a remarkably comprehensive survey of the career of Jesus, from being sent by God to work on earth to his ongoing work in heaven (see chapter 7 below). But Paul tells this story with frequent reference, for example, to the stories of creation, Adam, Abraham, Israel, and even Paul himself. In this section we briefly look at two examples of underlying stories in Romans: the story of creation and the fall in Romans 5–8[10] and the big story of the gospel that spans the entire letter.

The story of creation and the fall of humanity in Genesis 2–3 looms large in Paul's multifaceted teaching about sin and salvation in Romans 5, 7, and 8. Although these chapters are almost devoid of Old Testament quotations,[11] several allusions to texts in Genesis make this clear:

- The description of sin and death entering the world through one man's sin in Romans 5:12 is a clear allusion to Genesis 2:17; 3:6.
- Paul's description of his own struggle with sin in Romans 7:11 ("For sin, seizing an opportunity through the commandment,

9 See the survey in A. A. Das, "Narrative," in *DPL*[2] 718–21.

10 Cf. Thomas R. Schreiner, *Romans*, 2nd ed., BECNT (Grand Rapids, MI: Baker Academic, 2018), 256, on how Rom. 5:20; 6:14–15; and 7:1–24 show that "those who live under the law replicate the history of Adam and Israel, since commandments provide no ability to bear fruit for God."

11 Just two Old Testament quotations appear: Ex. 20:17 / Deut. 5:21 in Rom. 7:7; Ps. 44:22 in Rom. 8:36.

deceived [*exapataō*] me and through it killed me") recalls Genesis 3:13 ("The woman said, 'The serpent *deceived* [LXX: *apataō*] me, and I ate'"); Genesis 2:17 ("you shall surely die").

- Paul notes in Romans 8:20 that "the creation was subjected to futility," echoing the cursing of the ground that produced thorns and thistles and resulted in sweaty brows and painful toil in Genesis 3:17–19.

The critical role that stories play in Paul's exposition of the gospel in Romans can also be seen when we take a wide-angle view. Consider this panoramic sketch of the gospel narrative in Romans that underscores the role of the stories of creation and Israel in the story of Jesus:

> Paul begins with creation (1:20, 25; 3:30; 4:17; 11:26) and God's plan for humanity and God's own people (8:21, 29–30) in the face of wrath because of human sin since Adam (1:18–32; 5:12–21). God promised already to Abraham in Scripture a rescue operation targeting God's elect (4:13, 17; 9:6–24, 33; 10:19–21), a necessary operation since God's law had proven ineffectual (3:2, 19; 7:12–24). God's faithfulness and identity (3:21–26; 5:8; 8:31–35; 9:5) were ultimately revealed through the Son who suffered death (3:25; 4:25; 5:8; 7:24–25; 8:32; 14:15). The resurrection of the Son of God with power bears implications for God's own [people] (1:4; 4:17, 25; 6:4–5; 8:34; 10:9–13; 14:9). God calls Gentiles (1:17; 3:29–30; 4:5; 9:23–24; 15:9–12) and temporarily hardens Israel (3:3–4; 11:1–28). Ultimately, the faithful God will judge the world and be glorified (5:9; 8:18, 31–39; 12:19; 14:10–12; 15:9–12).[12]

The gospel in Romans has a long backstory and a wide story arc.

12 Das, "Narrative," 719–20, summarizing R. B. Hays, "The God of Mercy Who Rescues Us from the Present Evil Age: Romans and Galatians," in *The Forgotten God: Perspectives in Biblical Theology*, ed. A. A. Das and F. J. Matera (Louisville, KY: Westminster John Knox, 2002), 123–42.

Individual and Corporate Identity in Romans

Does Paul think of human beings in individual or corporate terms in Romans? Much recent Pauline scholarship argues that Paul is a communal thinker and may not even have a concept of the individual. Social-scientific approaches argue that in the first-century Mediterranean world "persons considered themselves in terms of the group(s) in which they experienced themselves as inextricably embedded."[13] Anti-individualism was also a key driver for the new perspective on Paul, with Paul's doctrine of justification understood as "primarily oriented toward the interpretation of the people of God" and union with Christ as "a communal concept."[14] A third anti-individualist trend in recent Pauline studies is the apocalyptic understanding of Paul, with its emphasis on the cosmic triumph of God at the heart of Paul's view of salvation. J. Louis Martyn, for example, argues that "the root antidote to an individual sin is not an individual instance of forgiveness . . . [but rather] vanquishing the enslaving power of Sin."[15]

However, it is more accurate to think of the individual and the community belonging together in Paul's thought. In terms of the history of ideas, Larry Siedentop's tour de force, *Inventing the Individual*, credits Christianity for the concept of humans as free agents, an essential notion for the very idea of a personal identity. According to Siedentop, in Paul's hands "the identity of individuals is no longer exhausted [as it once was] by the social roles they happen to occupy."[16] Paul had something to do with the very idea of the individual. There is no need to dismiss the importance of the individual in order to note the fundamentally communal context of his letters. While Paul knows nothing of an isolated

13 B. Malina, *The New Testament World: Insights from Cultural Anthropology* (Louisville, KY: Westminster John Knox, 2001), 62.

14 W. D. Davies, "Paul: From the Jewish Point of View," in *The Early Roman Period*, vol. 3 of *The Cambridge History of Judaism*, ed. W. D. Davies (Cambridge: Cambridge University Press, 1999), 716.

15 J. L. Martyn, *Galatians: A New Translation with Introduction and Commentary*, AB 33A (New York: Doubleday, 1997), 101.

16 L. Siedentop, *Inventing the Individual: The Origins of Western Liberalism* (Cambridge: Harvard University Press, 2014), 62.

individualism, his understanding of salvation in Christ is still deeply personal (see, e.g., Rom. 9:3; 1 Cor. 15:10; Gal. 6:17; Phil. 3:13–14).

Ben Dunson argues that Paul conceptualizes the individual in a wide variety of ways. In Romans, for instance, there are (1) *characteristic* individuals, such as the weak and the strong (Rom. 14:1–15:7), which Paul uses to urge individual action; (2) *generic* individuals (Rom. 2–3) to underscore the prospect of final judgment of every individual, both Jews and Gentiles; (3) *binary* individuals (Rom. 9–11) to stress the centrality of individual faith (see, e.g., 10:6–13); (4) *exemplary* individuals, such as David and Abraham (Rom. 4), whose examples of faith are commended; (5) *representative* individuals, such as Adam and Christ (Rom. 5), a sort of corporately determined individuality; (6) *somatic* individuals, the individual embedded within the believing community (Rom. 12); and (7) *particular* individuals (Rom. 16), each with a distinctive identity.[17] For Paul, there is no individual outside of community; equally, there is no community without individuals at the heart of the community's ongoing life. "The individual and the community are two sides of the same coin."[18]

Conclusion

The need for the gospel of God could not be more apparent. Human beings are under both the condemnation and dominion of sin. Rescue from this dire and desperate plight requires the gospel to be "the power of God for salvation" (1:16). Indeed, it was "while we were still weak" (5:6) that God acted decisively to save us. Jesus taught that "when a strong man, fully armed, guards his own palace," a "stronger" man is required for the work of liberation (Luke 11:21–22). It is to just such a powerful intervention that we now turn.

17 Ben C. Dunson, *Individual and Community in Paul's Letter to the Romans*, WUNT 2/332 (Tübingen: Mohr Siebeck, 2012).

18 Dunson, *Individual and Community in Paul's Letter to the Romans*, 15.

4

The Gospel of God's Saving Righteousness

Just and the justifier.

ROMANS 3:26

THE GOOD NEWS OF THE GOSPEL starts with the bad news of human "ungodliness and unrighteousness" (1:18), the inescapable "judgment of God" (2:3), and "the whole world [being] held accountable to God" (3:19). Indeed, nothing brings home the magnitude of a rescue like realizing the plight from which you have been delivered. Just when we learn of our certain condemnation in 1:18–3:20, Romans takes a dramatic turn: "But now" (3:21) God has done something to intervene: God declares righteous and redeems those who have faith in Jesus. The gospel tells the bleakest and brightest story in the world.[1]

What God has done and how he has done it is the subject of 3:21–31. It involves a *revelation* of his righteousness (3:21), taking our minds back to 1:16–17, where Paul declares that the righteousness of God is *revealed*

1 Parts of the first half of this chapter (up to "Salvation in Romans 4–16") are adapted from Brian S. Rosner, "The Revelation of God's Saving Righteousness: Romans 3:21–31," in *Paul's Letter to the Romans*, ed. Douglas J. Moo, Eckhard Schnabel, Frank Thielman, and Thomas R. Schreiner (Peabody, MA: Hendrickson Academic, 2023), 112–30. Used by permission.

in the gospel, and taking our minds forward to 16:25–26, where Paul's gospel and preaching of Jesus Christ are "according to the *revelation* of the mystery that was kept secret for long ages but has now been disclosed." Romans 3:21–31 is a central passage in the letter, so I will spend the first part of this chapter presenting a succinct exegesis of it, majoring on its contribution to the argument and theology of Romans. I will leave the subject of the witness of "the Law and the Prophets" to the gospel (3:21) until chapter 6 and say much more about the work of Christ in chapter 7.

The good news of justification and redemption in 3:21–26 is not, however, the only way in which Paul describes salvation in Romans. In the second half of this chapter, we will look at other teaching about salvation in the rest of Romans. I will have more to say about the agents of salvation in chapters 7 and 9 in connection with God's Son and God's Spirit, respectively. The human response to the gospel is the subject of chapter 5.

The Revelation of God's Saving Righteousness through Faith (3:21–31)

At the end of the thesis statement in Romans 1:16–17, Paul quotes Habakkuk 2:4: "The righteous shall live by faith." It is a perfectly chosen text for Romans because it is the only Old Testament verse that includes both righteousness and faith language, it is a response in its context to accusations against the character of God, and it concerns God's people "waiting in faith for the final revelation of God's salvation."[2] Paul uses it to underscore his message that "the righteous will only enjoy the life promised in the gospel by responding to the message with faith."[3]

Marcus Mininger notes that "the main point [of Romans 3:21–26] . . . is in the strong, opening affirmation that God's righteousness has now been revealed (v. 21), which is reiterated in verses 22, 25 and 26."[4]

2 Michael F. Bird, *Romans*, SGBC 6 (Grand Rapids, MI: Zondervan Academic, 2016), 44.

3 David G. Peterson, *Commentary on Romans*, BTCP (Nashville: Holman Reference, 2017), 107.

4 Marcus A. Mininger, *Uncovering the Theme of Revelation in Romans 1:16–3:26*, WUNT 445 (Tübingen: Mohr Siebeck, 2017), 357.

Arguably, the same theme extends to the end of Romans 3. The following exegesis of 3:21–31 underscores what each of the six subdivisions highlights about the revelation of God's saving righteousness.[5] In Romans 3:21–31, Paul asserts six key truths about the revelation of God's saving righteousness. It is

1. manifested in the new age (3:21–22b),
2. available to all (3:22c–24),
3. displayed in the death of Jesus Christ (3:25–26),
4. excludes boasting (3:27–28),
5. establishes God as the God of both Jews and Gentiles (3:29–30), and
6. confirms the prophetic role of the law (3:31).

Manifested in the New Age (3:21–22b)

Paul writes in Romans 3:21, "But now the righteousness of God has been manifested apart from the law, although the Law and the Prophets bear witness to it." As C. E. B. Cranfield notes, this "attestation of the gospel by the OT is of fundamental importance for Paul. [This] is indicated by the solemn way in which he insists on it here in what is one of the great hinge sentences on which the argument of the epistle turns."[6]

Romans 3:21 sets up a contrast between the failure of the law of Moses to save and the testimony of the Law and the Prophets to God's saving action in Christ. Many commentators take "apart from the law" to mean "apart from doing the law." But while it is true theologically that we are saved not by works—something Paul affirms elsewhere—the point here seems to be more than just this. It is not that righteousness is *received* apart from law but that righteousness is *disclosed* apart from law. Paul's "but now" signals a new stage of salvation history.

In 3:21 "law" (*nomos*) has the same referent in both sides of the contrast. The righteousness of God has been disclosed apart from the law

5 The outline is adapted from John D. Harvey, *Romans*, EGGNT (Nashville: B&H Academic, 2017), 100, 103–4.

6 C. E. B. Cranfield, *A Critical and Exegetical Commentary on the Epistle to the Romans: Introduction and Commentary on Romans 1–8*, ICC (London: T&T Clark, 1975), 203.

as law-covenant, but it is testified to by "the Law [and the Prophets]" *as prophecy* (see chapter 6 below). With this shift in salvation history, the law does not cease to be relevant. Rather, its function changes. Even if the law-covenant did not disclose the saving righteousness of God, it does (along with the Prophets) bear witness to it. The same point is made in 3:31, where Paul insists that the saving righteousness of God upholds the law as prophecy of the gospel.

The contrast is between 1:18–3:20 and 3:21–26, a shift from the old era to the new era. But it is important to understand the nature of the temporal shift. It is not that we move from the wrath of God to the righteousness of God. Paul affirms that the old era displayed God's forbearance (3:26). Rather, as D. A. Carson puts it, "The law covenant could not effect righteousness or ensure that anyone be declared righteous . . . , under the new era what is needed is righteousness that is manifested apart from the law."[7]

In 3:22 this saving righteousness of God comes "through the faith of Jesus Christ" (literal translation). The big question of course is whether "faith of Christ" (*pistis christou*) refers to faith in Christ or the faithfulness of Christ (see e.g., ESV and CEB, respectively)—that is, an objective or a subjective genitive. Or is it a deliberately ambiguous phrase, as Francis Watson argues, "pointing open-endedly, to the faith that pertains to God's saving action in Christ—originating it, participating in it, and oriented towards it"?[8] The arguments are ongoing.

Paul's unambiguously uses "faith" (*pistis*) and "believe" (*pisteuō*) in contexts of salvation, both in Romans and elsewhere, to refer to human belief and trust. The question then is whether the ambiguous use, "faith of Christ," is meant to reinforce these or supplement them with a reference to Christ's faithfulness. On balance, I favour taking *pistis christou* as an objective genitive in Romans 3:22: "faith in Jesus Christ."

7 D. A. Carson, "Atonement in Romans 3:21–26," in *The Glory of the Atonement: Biblical, Historical, and Practical Perspectives: Essays in Honor of Roger R. Nicole*, ed. Charles E. Hill and Frank A. James III (Downers Grove, IL: IVP Academic, 2004), 122.

8 Francis Watson, *Paul, Judaism and the Gentiles: Beyond the New Perspective* (Grand Rapids, MI: Eerdmans, 2007), 255.

Either way, little is at stake theologically, for Paul underscores the critical part played by the faithful obedience of Christ to our salvation (Rom. 5:12–21; Phil. 2:5–11), and he also commonly expresses the need for faith in Christ—not least in the following words in Romans 3:22. The argument that the reference to human faith in 3:22 makes the objective genitive interpretation redundant can cut both ways. One person's redundancy is another person's emphasis! (On the meaning of faith, see chapter 5 below.)

Available to All (3:22c–24)

Paul goes on to say that the saving righteousness of God is to the advantage (*eis* + the accusative) of "all" who exercise faith in Christ (3:22). In context the "all" is both believing Jews and believing Gentiles; "there is no distinction [or "difference" (*diastolē*)]." The only other place in Romans where this term occurs is a virtual commentary on its use in 3:22: "For there is no distinction between Jew and Greek; for the same Lord is Lord of all, bestowing his riches on all who call on him" (10:12). In 3:23–24 and 3:29–30, Paul redefines the Jewish idea of election—that only Abraham's children are God's chosen people.[9] Paul's explanation for God's impartiality is given in 3:23 in terms of the universality of human sin. It recalls Paul's argument in 1:18–3:20 and the concluding verdict that "all, both Jews and Greeks, are under sin" (3:9).

In 3:23 the consequence of human sin, taking the connective *kai* in the sense of "and so,"[10] is that human beings lack "the glory of God." This is probably a reference to the glory Adam lost when he transgressed in the garden, which applies to all people since all were in Adam when he fell (Rom. 5). The next reference to "the glory of God" is 5:2, which indicates that the blessings of salvation include a joyous restoration of that glory (cf. 8:30: "those whom he justified he also glorified").

Paul goes on in 3:24 to describe those who exercise faith in Christ and benefit from the saving righteousness of God. Using the terms

9 For more on this, see chap. 10.

10 Harvey, *Romans*, 92.

"grace" (*charis*) and "freely" (CSB, *dōrean*), Paul indicates that the saving righteousness of God has the character of a gift. More controversially, the salvation that God's saving righteousness brings is described in terms of justification (repeated in 3:26 and 3:28) and redemption, drawing on lawcourt and slave-market imagery respectively.

Usage in the LXX, usage in Paul's letters, and the context in Romans all point to the act of being justified (*dikaioō*) as having a forensic sense—that is, God's declaring in the present a verdict of acquittal and forgiveness, effectively a declaration of righteousness. God commands the judges of Israel (LXX Ex. 23:7; Isa. 5:22–23) to uphold justice and not to "acquit" (*dikaioō*) the "ungodly" (*asebēs*).[11] Most telling is the fact that in the LXX the verbs "to justify" and "to condemn" are frequently set in opposition to each other (e.g., LXX Deut. 25:1), a contrast that also appears in Romans 8:33–34.

Along with the vertical sense of being put right with God, there is a horizontal dimension to justification. As Romans 3:27–31 indicates, God is the God of both Jews and Gentiles. The blessings of justification include a new righteous status before God and being made part of a new people of God.[12] Romans 4 makes clear that justification by grace refers to God's generous kindness to the undeserving: "Now to the one who works, his wages are not counted as a gift but as his due" (Rom. 4:4; cf. Eph. 2:8–9; 2 Tim. 1:9).[13] Furthermore, Romans 4 includes both aspects of grace—(1) undeserved favor to all and (2) the incorporation of both Jews and Gentiles in the one new family of God.

The agency through which justification is made possible is "redemption" (3:24). The notion of redemption is common in Paul and is associated with the forgiveness of sins, release from captivity, and the payment of a ransom in various contexts. While we should avoid lumping all these meanings into every occurrence of the word (the

11 Cf. 4:5: God "justifies the ungodly."

12 The two halves of Eph. 2 (Eph. 2:1–10 and 2:11–22) similarly expound the vertical and horizontal dimensions of salvation.

13 Cf. I. H. Marshall, "Salvation, Grace and Works in the Later Writings in the Pauline Corpus," *NTS* 42, no. 3 (1996): 339–58.

fallacy of illegitimate totality transfer), there are good grounds to take redemption in the broadest sense in 3:24. The Old Testament background has both freedom from slavery and the payment of a price in view. Such fits well in the context of 3:23–24. As Schreiner notes, "The contrast between 'freely' and the redemption provided by God suggests that the latter includes the idea of a price being paid."[14] Additionally, sacrificial overtones are present in the terms "mercy seat" (*hilastērion*, ESV: "propitiation") and "blood" in 3:25.

The redemption takes place "in Christ Jesus," pointing either to its spatial location or its source[15]—or, better, "in association with Christ Jesus" as Constantine Campbell argues.[16] All three are true elsewhere, according to Paul. As is often the case in exegesis of Romans 3:21–26, the question is not whether Paul says something in his letters but, rather, whether he says it here in this letter.

A powerful illustration of the wide reach of the gospel that is available to all is Paul's lengthy greetings to the Roman Christians in Romans 16. As Michael Gorman notes, the list "embodies the Pauline vision of an inclusive community: gentiles and Jews; slave, free, and freedpersons; elite and non-elite; men and women; from all corners of the empire."[17] Based on scholarly research on the names in 16:1–15 and their possible backgrounds, Paul greets sixteen men and seven women (at least six from a Jewish background) and around ten slaves or former slaves.[18]

Displayed in the Death of Jesus Christ (3:25–26)

In 3:25–26, an extended relative clause "describes the details of how God is able to declare sinners righteous without violating his own

14 Thomas R. Schreiner, *Romans,* 2nd ed., BECNT (Grand Rapids, MI: Baker Academic, 2018), 198.

15 Richard N. Longnecker, *Epistle to the Romans* (Grand Rapids, MI: Eerdmans, 2016), 424.

16 Constantine R. Campbell, *Paul and Union with Christ: An Exegetical and Theological Study* (Grand Rapids, MI: Zondervan Academic, 2012), 74.

17 Michael J. Gorman, *Romans: A Theological and Pastoral Commentary* (Grand Rapids, MI: Eerdmans, 2022), 294.

18 Cf. Gorman, *Romans,* 293–94.

righteousness."[19] First, God publicly displayed Christ as a *hilastērion*—that is, as either a propitiation, expiation, sacrifice of atonement, place of atonement, or mercy seat. Chapter 7 will look at this term in some detail. I conclude tentatively that "mercy seat" is the best translation.[20]

God's purpose in displaying Jesus as the mercy seat by his blood is to demonstrate his righteousness. How does it do this? God's righteous character might have been called into question since he had passed over sins without punishing them prior to the sacrifice of Christ. But the death of Christ vindicates God's righteous character in the present era, "showing that the forgiveness granted did not compromise his justice";[21] thus, God remains righteous when he declares as righteous those who believe in Jesus.

A possible weakness with this interpretation of 3:25–26 is that the demonstration of God's righteousness is his judging righteousness rather than his saving righteousness. However, "the righteousness of God" appears in 3:5 as God's judging righteousness and the cognate term in 2:5, *dikaiokrisia*, refers to God's "just/fair verdict"[22] in punishing sinners. And as Schreiner points out, "the presence of δίκαιον [*dikaion*; in 3:26] indicates that God's righteousness can't be confined to his saving righteousness."[23] In other words, not only God's saving righteousness but also his judging righteousness are displayed in the death of Christ.

Excludes Boasting (3:27–28)

Paul's exposition of the saving righteousness of God in 3:21–26 as manifested in the new age, available to all without distinction, and displayed in the death of Christ raises questions concerning the role of the law of Moses—something Paul mentions in 3:21. The revelation of the saving righteousness of God has implications for the role of the law. In short,

19 Harvey, *Romans*, 93.

20 The two occurrences of *hilastērion* in the New Testament are Rom. 3:24 and Heb. 9:5, where the ESV translates it as "propitiation" and "mercy seat," respectively.

21 Schreiner, *Romans*, 204.

22 "Δικαιοκρισία," in BDAG 246.

23 Schreiner, *Romans*, 206.

Romans 3:27–31 picks up on the critical nature of faith in the justification of both Jews and Gentiles, a theme introduced in 3:22 and 3:26.

In 3:27–28 the revelation of God's saving righteousness excludes boasting. It does this in two ways: through the law of faith (3:27) and because God justifies people by faith apart from works (3:28).

First, boasting is excluded not by a "law of works" but by a "law of faith" (3:27). Some interpreters understand the law of faith and the law of works as two different ways of using the law of Moses. Understood in terms of works, the law leads to boasting; understood in terms of faith, it does not. However, as Douglas Moo argues, at this point in Romans Paul has made the law and faith mutually exclusive. Paul's discussions in 3:21–26 and 3:28 are what lead him to ask, "Do we then overthrow the law by this faith?" (3:31). "This question does not make sense unless Paul has, in this context, fully separated 'faith' from the law of Moses."[24] Indeed, the distinction between doing and believing, with the former aligned with the law, is maintained throughout Romans (see 2:25–29; 3:2; 4:2–8; 9:31–10:8).

It is better to understand Paul contrasting two different "laws" in 3:27. The referent to "law of works," as Moo puts it, "would naturally bring to mind *the* law, the torah."[25] Paul has forged such a link between the law and works in Romans (see 2:6–16, 25–27; 3:20) that the connection may be assumed. Thus, with the contrast between "the law of faith" and "the law of works," Paul asserts that "the characteristic demand of the Mosaic covenant—works—is contrasted with the basic demand of the New Covenant—faith."[26] The "law of faith," as Thielman suggests, may even refer to the new covenant.[27]

Second, boasting is excluded because "one is justified by faith apart from works of the law" (3:28, repeating a point Paul made in 3:20). "Works of the law" (*erga nomou*) is best taken to be Paul's shorthand

24 Douglas J. Moo, *The Letter to the Romans*, 2nd ed., NICNT (Grand Rapids, MI: Eerdmans, 2018), 248.

25 Moo, *Romans*, 249.

26 Moo, *Romans*, 250.

27 Frank Thielman, *Paul and the Law: A Contextual Approach* (Downers Grove, IL: InterVarsity Press, 1994), 183.

for "doing what the law requires,"[28] which can take on different nuances in different contexts.

But what sort of boasting is excluded? Given the broader context of Romans, the emerging answer is that Paul opposes both the idea of salvation by good works and Jewish privilege. In Romans 2:17 and 2:23, Paul mentions Israel's boast in the law and in the knowledge of God, which they believe grants them a status above the Gentiles.[29] And in 4:2 Paul pits faith and doing against one another as opposing ways of obtaining the righteousness of God.

Establishes God as the God of Both Jews and Gentiles (3:29–30)

Romans 3:29 opens with the word "or" introducing a second implication of the revelation of the saving righteousness of God—namely, it establishes God as the God of both Jews and Gentiles. In short, the fact that there is one God means that there is one way of salvation for all people.

"God is one" (3:30) is an allusion to the Shema (see Deut. 6:4). The oneness of God is connected in the Old Testament to God's covenant with Israel. But Paul subverts this association by also alluding to Zechariah 14:9: "The Lord will be king over all the earth. On that day the Lord will be one and his name one."

In describing Jews as "the circumcised" and Gentiles as "the uncircumcised" (3:30), Paul hints that faith, not Jewish privilege or performance, is critical for being part of God's family. Both Jews and Gentiles are justified by faith.

28 See Thomas R. Schreiner, *New Testament Theology: Magnifying God in Christ* (Grand Rapids, MI: Baker Academic, 2008), 527. For a survey of the interpretation of "works of law," see Schreiner, *New Testament Theology*, 526–27. Cf. Michael F. Bird, *The Saving Righteousness of God: Studies in Paul, Justification, and the New Perspective* (Eugene, OR: Wipf and Stock, 2007), 98, who defines the phrase as "a metonym for the stipulations of the entire Mosaic code" and notes that such works are "just as much *ethical* as they are *ethnic*" (emphasis in original). Bird also offers a convincing critique of the attempts of James D. G. Dunn and N. T. Wright to limit the phrase to those laws that functioned as boundary markers between Jews and Gentiles (i.e., circumcision, Sabbath keeping, and dietary regulations). Bird, *The Saving Righteousness of God*, 96–99.

29 Simon J. Gathercole, *Where Is Boasting? Early Jewish Soteriology and Paul's Response in Romans 1–5* (Grand Rapids, MI: Eerdmans, 2002), 225.

Confirms the Prophetic Role of the Law (3:31)

Paul brings 3:21–31 to a climax by answering an objection. When righteousness is manifested apart from the law-covenant for both Jews and Gentiles, does Paul's emphasis on faith in the new era of universal salvation abolish the law altogether? "Do we then overthrow [*katargeō*] the law by this faith? By no means! On the contrary, we uphold the law [*alla nomon histanomen*]" (Rom. 3:31).

Paul denies that this new thing God has done in the sacrificial death of Christ (3:25) does away with the law. It is not that Christians end up "under the law" after all. Paul, as Carson puts it, "does not uphold *nomos* ("law") as *lex*, as ongoing legal demand."[30] Rather, the law is upheld—that is, "validated" and its "validity reinforced" (*histēmi*)[31]—not *as commandments in the new age* but *as prophecy of the new age* in which both Jews and Gentiles will be justified by grace through faith. Paul abolishes the law as law-covenant but upholds it as prophecy.[32]

The upholding of the law (3:31) is, in effect,

> the unpacking of the last clause of Romans 3:21: the Law and the Prophets testify to this new "righteousness from God" that has come in Christ Jesus, and thus their valid continuity is sustained in that to which they point. . . . The law is upheld precisely because the redemptive-historical purposes and anticipations of the law are upheld.[33]

The connection of Romans 3:31 with 3:21 is given more credence when it is recognized that 4:1–25 is effectively an exposition of Genesis 15:6 from the Law and Psalm 32:1–2 from the Prophets.

30 Carson, "Atonement in Romans 3:21–26," 139.

31 See "ἵστημι," in BDAG 482.

32 See Brian S. Rosner, *Paul and the Law: Keeping the Commandments of God*, NSBT 31 (Downers Grove: IVP Academic, 2013). Cf. Joseph A. Fitzmyer, *Romans: A New Translation with Introduction and Commentary*, AB 33 (New York: Doubleday, 1993), 367: "In insisting on faith as the one principle of salvation, and in linking it to the one God, Paul affirms the basic message of the OT, and in particular that of the Mosaic law itself, rightly understood."

33 Carson, "Atonement in Romans 3:21–26," 139.

Salvation in Romans 4–16

Since the contents of the gospel are the identity and work of Jesus Christ (1:1–6) and its main function is to save those who believe (1:16–17), Paul uses many terms and images for the deliverance it achieves. In Romans 3:21–26, to be saved is to be justified and redeemed. In this section, we explore the teaching of Romans on these and other terms. The umbrella idea, or "governing motif"[34] under which they all sit, is the general notion of salvation, denoting a "rescue from danger . . . to a state of safety and well being."[35]

In Romans, to be saved is to be justified, forgiven, counted as righteous, redeemed, set free, adopted into God's family, reconciled, united to Christ, made holy, given eternal life, and granted honor and glory. In many cases these ideas of salvation overlap in meaning. Most of them have both present and future dimensions; they are true already but not yet fully realized. Most flow seamlessly into Paul's teaching on Christian conduct, a point to which we shall return in chapter 11. Most are explicitly associated with the person and work of Jesus Christ as their ground or source. Each addresses different aspects of our plight and predicament (see table 4.1).

Table 4.1 Ideas of Salvation in Romans

Idea of salvation	Ground / source	Plight / predicament
Salvation	The death and risen life of Christ (5:8–10)	"The wrath of God" (5:9)
Justification	"Through our Lord Jesus Christ" (5:1)	Condemnation (8:1)
Forgiveness	Jesus was "delivered up for [the forgiveness of] our trespasses" (4:25)	The penalty of sin (1:18)
Imputation	Righteousness in Christ (4:3–5; 5:17)	Condemnation in Adam (5:12–21)

34 Mark J. Keown, *Romans and the Mission of God* (Eugene, OR: Wipf and Stock, 2021), 114.

35 "Σῴζω; σωτηρία," in L&N 241 (21.18).

Table 4.1 (*continued*)

Idea of salvation	Ground / source	Plight / predicament
Redemption	"In Christ Jesus" (3:24)	Slavery to sin (6:6, 16)
Freedom	"In Christ Jesus" (8:2)	Slavery to sin (6:6, 16)
Adoption	Receiving "the Spirit of adoption" (8:15)	"The spirit of slavery [to sin]" (8:15)
Reconciliation	"By the death of [God's] Son" (5:10)	Enemies of God (5:10)
Union with Christ	By dying and rising with Christ (6:3–4)	Being in Adam (5:12–19)
Holiness	"Into Christ Jesus" (6:1–4, 19)	Impurity (6:19)
Eternal life	"In Christ Jesus our Lord" (6:23)	"The wages of sin is death" (6:23)
Glory and honor	"Through our Lord Jesus Christ" (5:1–2)	Shame (6:21) and falling short of God's glory (3:23)

Salvation

The importance of the idea of salvation in Romans is made clear in the thesis statement in 1:16–17, where Paul states that the gospel is "the power of God for salvation." The broad nature of the idea of salvation in Romans is borne out by its presence throughout the letter and its association with four other images of deliverance: justification, reconciliation, adoption, and redemption. Building on the argument of Romans 1–3, Paul's next use of salvation language is in 5:9–10 where we are saved by Jesus's death and risen life "from the wrath of God" (5:9). Here, salvation is the outcome of justification and reconciliation. Then, in 8:24 salvation is future oriented (cf. 13:11): We are saved by God (a divine passive) in the hope of our adoption and the redemption of our bodies. Finally, in 10:9–10, salvation—by confessing the lordship of the risen Jesus—is again associated with justification.[36]

36 Salvation language also appears in the context of Paul's desire for the Jews to be saved in 9:27; 10:1, 9, 10, 13; 11:11, 14, 26.

Justification

Justification in Romans is directly related to the theme of the righteousness of God. In chapter 1 we looked in brief at the *dik*- language in Romans and noted how the whole letter can be outlined in relation to God's saving righteousness in the gospel. Justification (as noted above in relation to 3:24, 26) has a forensic sense, meaning God declares sinners righteous on the basis of the death of Christ. Justification is achieved not only by God displaying Jesus's death as the mercy seat (3:25) but also by Jesus's resurrection—Jesus our Lord was "raised for the purpose of securing our justification" (4:25 my translation).[37] In Romans 4 (quoting Gen. 15:6 and Ps. 32:1–2), Abraham and David are forgiven and declared righteous by faith. If a righteous status is conferred in Romans 4, similarly in 5:17 righteousness is reified and offered as a gift, received by faith. Romans 8–10 also use righteousness language for the righteous status declared at justification (see 8:10; 9:30–31; 10:3, 4, 5, 6, 10). Furthermore, being declared righteous is to lead to righteous behavior: Believers are to present themselves as "instruments for righteousness" (6:13); believers are "slaves to righteousness" (6:18–19); and righteousness is behavior appropriate to the kingdom of God (14:17).

Forgiveness

Forgiveness of sins is related to justification. Forgiveness is a necessary part of being declared righteous. Paul declares the blessedness of "those whose lawless deeds are forgiven, / and whose sins are covered" (Rom. 4:7, quoting Ps. 32:1). Kindred thoughts appear elsewhere: Christ was "delivered up for [the forgiveness of] our trespasses" (Rom. 4:25), and believers are "set free from [the penalty and power of] sin" (6:7, 18, 22). Indeed, a key promise of the new covenant is that God takes away our sins (Rom. 11:27).

37 Just as Jesus is himself "justified/vindicated" by God at his resurrection (see Rom. 1:3–4; Acts 2:36; 1 Tim. 3:16) so too we are justified/vindicated as those who are in union with Christ. Bird, *Romans*, 152: "We are incorporated into the justification of Jesus the Messiah in his resurrection."

Imputation

Some Reformed theologians hold that there are two sides to our justification—namely, Christ's passive obedience (his death for our sins) and active obedience (his perfect obedience to the law). Our sin is imputed to Christ, he bears it on the cross, and his obedient life of righteousness is imputed to us. However, some biblical scholars object that Paul nowhere says that the righteousness of Christ is imputed to believers. The relevant texts in Romans are 4:3–5 and 5:12–21 (cf. 1 Cor. 1:30; 2 Cor. 5:19–21; Gal. 2:20; Phil. 3:8–9). The debate can be settled by distinguishing between the tasks of exegesis and theology. Theology is a synthesising discipline; thus, not every point of theology can be explicitly supported by biblical proof texts. In my view, the imputation of Christ's righteousness is a logical and necessary inference resting on several biblical ideas. These include the representative nature of Adam and Christ, Christ's obedience and faithfulness, righteousness as a gift (Rom. 5:17), and the commercial language of reckoning/imputing (4:3–5). When we are justified by grace, we stand before God not only forgiven but also reckoned as righteous through our union with Christ.

Redemption

There are two references to redemption in Romans. The first is in 3:24 (discussed above)—"justified by his grace as a gift, through the redemption that is in Christ Jesus"—in which redemption is a global reference to our costly emancipation from the penalty and power of sin. The second reference is 8:23: "We wait eagerly for adoption as sons, the redemption of our bodies." This text has future and final freedom from sin and death in view. Together, these two verses reflect an already / not yet tension of present experience and full consummation of our status as God's sons (both men and women) and our bodily existence following Christ's return.

Freedom

A consequence of being redeemed is that believers, as manumitted slaves, are set free: "You have been set free [by God] from [the dominion and consequences of] sin and have become slaves of God" (6:22; cf. 6:18). Just as a widow is set free from the law of marriage when her husband dies (7:3) so also the believer, having died with Christ, has been "set . . . free in Christ Jesus from the law of sin and death" (8:2). In 8:21 the theme is extended beyond the emancipation of believers: "The creation itself will be set free from its bondage to corruption and obtain the freedom of the glory of the children of God." The salvation idea of freedom not only develops the image of redemption but also overlaps with honor, glory, and adoption.

Adoption

The family of God is Paul's fundamental metaphor for God's people, especially in Romans where God is referred to as Father four times and Christ the Son of God seven times.[38] The first item in Paul's list of Israelite privileges under the old covenant is adoption into God's family (9:4). Unsurprisingly, a major image for salvation for believers in Christ is also adoption. Believers are addressed as "brothers and sisters" sixteen times and individual believers as "brother or sister" four times in the letter.[39] Being part of God's family now, we cry out to God as our Father (8:15) and also eagerly await the full manifestation of our sonship in the future (8:23; cf. 8:19). Believers are "predestined to be conformed to the image of his Son, in order that he might be the firstborn among many brothers [and sisters]" (8:29). The plight for which adoption is the solution is described as having "the spirit of slavery [to sin] . . . [resulting in] fear" (8:15)—slavery to sin being typical of the old era in Romans 6 and 8. Sonship is not just an honorable status guaranteeing an inheritance (8:17) but also enables God's children to "put to death the deeds of the body" by the Spirit (8:13). "Those adopted are not enslaved to sin."[40]

38 Cf. Keown, *Romans and the Mission of God*, 133. On the metaphor of adoption, see Brian S. Rosner, *Known by God: A Biblical Theology of Personal Identity*, BTFL (Grand Rapids, MI: Zondervan Academic, 2017), 154–62.

39 See, e.g., ESV margin note on Rom. 9:3.

40 Schreiner, *Romans*, 418.

Reconciliation

While redemption uses the imagery of slavery, reconciliation is a relational metaphor. Justification brings peace with God (5:1), and that peace characterizes our reconciliation with God, where we move from enmity towards God to amity with him, achieved by the death and risen life of his Son (5:10). The extension of the offer of salvation to Gentiles leads to "the reconciliation of the world" (11:15), a restored relationship with God for all kinds of people across the world. Peace with God also leads to peace among the new people of God (14:17, 19). Indeed, reconciliation is the work of "the God of peace" (15:33; 16:20), who is the source of peace and harmony.

Union with Christ

Common in Romans, the language of "in Christ" (13x) and "in the Lord" (8x) is used in a variety of ways. Those that relate to salvation indicate that we identify with, are incorporated into, and participate in Christ's person and work such that he represents those that put their faith in him. In this way, Christ's death is our death to sin's penalty and power, and his resurrection is the source of our new life (6:3–4). We are alive to God in him (6:11), have eternal life through our union with him (6:23), escape condemnation in him (8:1), and are redeemed by him (3:24). Being in Christ and having him as our representative head is the only escape from being in Adam and his legacy of trespass, judgment, and condemnation (5:12–20; see chapter 7 for Christ dying as our representative). The love of God is expressed in Christ's work on our behalf (8:39). We are also one body in him (12:5) and hence greet fellow believers "in the Lord" (16:2, 8, 22).

Holiness

Regularly in Romans, Paul describes believers as *hagioi*, "holy ones" or "saints" (Rom. 1:7; 8:27; 12:13; 15:25, 31; 16:2, 15), those consecrated to the service of God.[41] Although holiness is not a focus

41 "Ἅγιος," in BDAG 11.

of Romans, the basis of this holy status is union with Christ Jesus (1 Cor. 1:30). In Romans 6:19 the position of being holy leads to the process of becoming holy: "Offer yourselves as slaves to righteousness leading to holiness" (NIV). This reflects the logic of Paul's teaching on Christian conduct more generally, that believers are to live in accordance with their new identity in Christ (see chapter 11 below) to become what they already are in Christ.

Eternal Life

In Romans 1:23, the "immortal [*aphthartos*] God" is contrasted with "mortal [*phthartos*] man," a description of human beings repeated in 6:12 and 8:11. However, that we are destined to die is not the natural state of affairs but, rather, the result of the passions of our bodies in disobedience to God (6:12) and the wages of our sin (6:23). Salvation, then, is "the free gift of God . . . in Christ Jesus our Lord" (6:23) coming through his resurrection from the dead (8:11). Union with Christ is the means by which eternal life is possible, and the character of that life is that it is lived in union with Christ.[42] As Keown states, "From an individualistic point of view, immortality is the ultimate outcome of the gospel."[43] Once again, however, salvation goes beyond the individual believer: The creation itself will also be set free from decay and death (8:21).

Glory and Honor

Although God is full of glory and honor (6:4; 9:23; 16:27), human beings fail to glorify God (1:21) and fall short of his glory (3:23). Salvation, then, requires the restoration to glory of those who believe in Christ (5:2; 8:21, 30; cf. 2:10) and a full experience of God's glory in the age to come (8:18). Another way of referring to receiving glory and honor is not being put to shame, something believers in Christ are also promised will never happen to them (Rom. 9:33, quoting Isa. 28:16).

42 David Abernathy, *An Exegetical Summary of Romans 1–8*, 2nd ed. (Dallas: SIL International, 2008), 444.

43 Keown, *Romans and the Mission of God*, 135; cf. 2:7: "he will give eternal life."

Conclusion

Paul describes the gospel of salvation in Romans from many angles. Like a treasure hunter who has discovered a stash of jewels, the apostle is eager to show us each and every one, and he holds them up to the light in turn to display their brilliant splendor. When it comes to talking about salvation, the language of "more than that" (5:11) resonates throughout the letter. In 5:1–11 Paul moves from justification (5:1, 9) to salvation (5:9) to reconciliation (5:11): "*More than that*, we also rejoice in God through our Lord Jesus Christ, through whom we have now received reconciliation."[44] Not only does the gospel offer deliverance from the wrath of God, the penalty of sin, and our deserved condemnation, "more than that" it also frees us from slavery to sin, turns us from God's enemies to his friends, makes us God's beloved children, and grants us honor and glory. There is no problem with preaching the gospel from one particular angle, such as justification or redemption. But to be strengthened by the gospel, we need them all. And just as the gospel of salvation can be variously described so too responding to the gospel can be expressed in several complementary ways.

44 Roy E. Ciampa, "Paul's Theology of the Gospel," in *Paul as Missionary: Identity, Activity, Theology, and Practice*, ed. Trevor J. Burke and Brian S. Rosner, LNTS 420 (Edinburgh: T&T Clark, 2011), 186, points out that "in 5:9–10 salvation is described as something that goes beyond justification. . . . It includes the newly empowered life that comes to those who have been raised from spiritual death."

5

Responding to the Gospel

The Obedience of Faith.

ROMANS 1:5; 16:26

IN ROMANS THERE ARE TWO WAYS of seeking to be "justified in [God's] sight" (3:20). The first is "by works of the law" (3:20) / "by works" (4:2) or—put another way—by seeking to establish your own righteousness (10:3). Paul could not be more emphatic about such attempts: "No human being will be justified" in this way (3:20)! The second way is to be "justified by [God's] grace as a gift . . . [through] faith in Jesus" (3:24–26). In this chapter, I examine the teaching of Romans on how to respond to the gospel of salvation. A number of questions need to be addressed, including the nature of grace and the meaning of faith.

The Nature of Grace

The grounds of salvation in Romans are "the abundance of grace [*charis*] and the free gift [*dōrea*] of righteousness" (Rom. 5:17). If we are "justified by [God's] grace" (Titus 3:7) "through Jesus Christ our Savior" (Titus 3:6) the corollary is that we are saved "not because of works done by us in righteousness" (Titus 3:5).[1] Understanding the grace of

1 Cf. Israel being told that their election by God was "not because of your righteousness" (Deut. 9:5, 6).

God in the gospel is critical for grasping how we are meant to respond to the gospel.

John Barclay's study of the variegated meanings of grace and gifts in Jewish and Greco-Roman culture in Paul's day provides some helpful categories and distinctions for our study of the grace of God in Romans.[2] Saying that salvation is a gift doesn't tell you much. A gift can be large or small, deserved or undeserved, given in response to a prior gift or with strings attached. Barclay's fresh terminology helps to illuminate a rich, complex, and familiar concept. God's grace is superabundant, antecedent, incongruous, and efficacious. And it demands and produces lives of obedience.

The grace of God is *superabundant* in its scale, significance, and duration. This is best seen in Romans 5:12–21 (*charis* appears 5x) where Paul contrasts the legacy of Adam with that of Christ and concludes that "the free gift [of Christ] is not like the trespass [of Adam]" (5:15). To underscore the difference between the two, Paul speaks of how "*much more* have the grace of God and the free gift by the grace of that one man Jesus Christ *abounded* for many" (5:15). Along with describing grace as superior and abundant, Paul says it "overflow[s]" and has "multiplied" (Rom. 5:17, 20 CSB). Elsewhere, Paul gives thanks for the "surpassing grace of God . . . his inexpressible gift" (2 Cor. 9:14–15). The grace of God in Romans is "huge, lavish, unceasing, [and] long-lasting."[3]

The timing of the gift of God's grace points to it being *antecedent* to any action on the part of recipients. Some gifts are in response to a preceding action or gift for the giver, making the gift in some sense an act of reciprocity. But the grace of God is without the prior initiative of the recipients; God is the sole initiator of the gift relationship. In Romans, Paul points to God's gracious act of creation as calling for thanksgiving (1:21), an act that clearly was not in response to anything that humans had done. God's election of Israel, "chosen by grace" (11:5), and his "irrevocable" gifts to the nation (11:29; cf. 3:1–2; 9:1–5) likewise

2 John M. G. Barclay, *Paul and the Gift* (Grand Rapids, MI: Eerdmans, 2015); John M. G. Barclay, *Paul and the Power of Grace* (Grand Rapids, MI: Eerdmans, 2020).

3 Barclay, *Paul and the Power of Grace*, 13.

affirm the giver as the initiator of the gift relationship. Jacob is an illustration of antecedent grace as it was given to one "not yet born" (9:11).

The attribute of the grace of God that receives the most attention in Romans is its *incongruity,* Barclay's term for the unmerited nature of grace. Some gifts have an element of reward or at least desert: Children are taught to expect big Christmas presents and not lumps of coal if they have been good boys and girls. God's grace is not only lavish and given in advance but is also supplied "without regard to the worth of the recipient."[4] That human beings do not deserve the gift of grace is hammered home in 1:18–3:20: "No one seeks for God. . . . No one does good, not even one" (3:11–12). Grace is granted to "the ungodly" (4:5), "sinners" (5:8), and the "enemies" of God (5:10)—not "on the basis of works; otherwise grace would no longer be grace" (11:6). Romans 9–11 makes clear that the calling of Israel also has nothing to do with the nation's moral worth or inherent value (cf., e.g., Deut. 7:6–9). Paul uses several roughly synonymous terms for "grace" in Romans that reinforce the lesson that God's grace is undeserved and motivated by his gracious character. God's motive in saving us is his love (Rom. 1:7; 5:5, 8; 8:35, 37), mercy (9:15, 16, 18, 23; 11:30, 31, 32; 15:9), compassion (9:15), and kindness (2:4; 11:22).

The epitome of grace for Paul was the admission of Gentiles—people "who did not seek" God (Rom. 10:20, quoting Isa. 65:1) and who were without God or hope (Eph. 2:12)—to the glorious privileges that had been exclusive to Israel. Living "under [the indiscriminate] grace" of God (Rom. 6:15) is the basis for Paul's vision of Christian community in Romans 12–14, since it undercuts the normal systems of value that divide human beings along ethnic, social, and cultural lines. The gift of God in the gospel "is, and remains always, incongruous—*a gift created out of human nothingness* and received in trust."[5] Throughout Romans, the death of Christ, "the grace of that one man" (5:15), is the ultimate expression of the grace of God.

4 Barclay, *Paul and the Gift*, 73.

5 Barclay, *Paul and the Power of Grace*, 86 (emphasis in original).

The antecedent and incongruous grace of God is *efficacious* in that "it infallibly accomplishes what God intends it to accomplish."[6] Some gifts achieve something and are not simply put on display or into storage. Grace puts us right with God. Christians "stand" in grace (5:2) and live "under grace" (6:15). Paul wishes believers an ongoing experience of (1:7; 16:20) and "access" to God's grace (5:2). He uses the word "grace" of his apostolic ministry to Gentiles as a gift from God (1:5; 15:15) and of the various abilities that God gives to his people (12:3, 6). Paul sees the grace of God as a gift that effects change not just in our status and destiny but also in our lives and world (see chapters 11–13 below). As Frank Thielman insists, "Grace is an overwhelming power that gives believers the ability to live righteous lives."[7] The nature of grace in Romans—free and demanding, liberating and transformative—can be seen in the opening chapters. In 2:6–10 we see that efficacious grace means that "those who have been transformed by the gift will have something to show for it on the day of judgment."[8]

A related point is that the grace of God *demands and produces lives of obedience* in the sense that "it is given in expectation of a response,"[9] and this response is also facilitated and enabled by God's grace. Barclay explains:

> The grace of God is designed to produce obedient lives that, by a transformative heart-inscription performed by the Spirit, produce what is pleasing to God. This grace justifies the ungodly but its purpose is not to leave them that way. In this sense, the grace of God is *unconditioned* (given in the absence of merit or worth) but not *unconditional,* if by that we mean without expectation or alteration in the recipients of the gift. It is free in the sense that it is without

6 Douglas J. Moo, *A Theology of Paul and His Letters: The Gift of the New Realm in Christ*, BTNT (Grand Rapids, MI: Zondervan Academic, 2021), 519.

7 Frank Thielman, "Adam's Sin and Jesus' Death in Romans 5:12–21," in *Paul's Letter to the Romans: Theological Essays*, ed. Douglas J. Moo, Eckhard Schnabel, Frank Thielman, and Thomas R. Schreiner (Peabody, MA: Hendrickson Academic, 2023), 146.

8 Barclay, *Paul and the Power of Grace*, 87.

9 Moo, *A Theology of Paul and His Letters*, 520.

> prior conditions; and it remains always a miraculous, conditioned gift forged out of human incapacity. But it is not free (or "cheap") in the sense that it expects no transformative result.[10]

This raises the question of where obedience fits in Paul's gospel in Romans. Is obedience part of the human response to the gospel? The answer would seem to be yes, given that Paul's stated goal in preaching the gospel is to "bring about the obedience of faith" (1:5). However, the meaning of this phrase is disputed. Does Paul mean "the obedience that comes from faith" (NIV) or the obedience that consists of faith (i.e., obedience to the gospel call to have faith in Jesus). Or does Paul mean both at the same time? Good arguments can be put forward for each of these interpretations. Obedience to God does flow from accepting the gospel: "As *obedient slaves* . . . [you] have become *obedient* from the heart to the standard of teaching to which you were committed" (6:16–17). And accepting the gospel can be described as an act of obedience: "They have not all *obeyed* the gospel" (10:16). In the end, deciding the precise meaning of the phrase is not critical, for, as Schreiner notes,

> Faith and obedience shouldn't be sundered as if Christians could have the former without the latter. When Paul reflects on his mission in Rom. 15:18, he remarks on "the obedience of the gentiles" showing that a changed lordship occurs for those who embrace the gospel. True faith always results in obedience. Paul also argues in Rom. 6 and 8 that the grace given in Christ invariably effects a transformation of one's everyday life (cf. also 12:1–13:14). . . . All obedience is rooted in and flows from faith.[11]

This in no way dilutes or sullies the unmerited (or to use Barclay's terms, unconditioned and incongruous) nature of God's grace. Salvation

10 Barclay, *Paul and the Power of Grace*, 87 (emphasis in original).

11 Thomas R. Schreiner, *Romans*, 2nd ed., BECNT (Grand Rapids, MI: Baker Academic, 2018), 40.

is a free gift received by faith, and this same salvation by grace through faith leads to a life of obedience to God. In chapter 11 we look at how God enables this transformation through union with Christ, the inspiring example of Christ, and life in the Spirit.

The Meaning of Faith

Paul uses the noun "faith" (*pistis*) 140 times and the verb "believe" or "to have faith" (*pisteuō*) 54 times in his letters. Romans dominates this usage with 40 occurrences of "faith" and 21 of "believe." The thesis statement of the letter (1:16–17) uses the words 4 times alone! In Romans the human response to the gospel is summed up by the idea of faith. Faith is "the disposition toward Christ and the gospel that God requires of his people."[12] The promise of salvation rests on grace, and being saved depends on faith (4:16).

Like *righteousness/justification* and *grace*, *faith* is a key term in the theology of Romans that requires careful definition. Fortunately, faith is not the only way that Paul describes the appropriate human response to the offer of salvation, and the synonyms for faith in Romans add to our understanding of the subject. Sinners are not only saved through faith in Jesus but also by repentance, confessing the name of the Lord, calling on the name of the Lord, receiving God's grace and gift, putting one's hope in the Messiah, and baptism. These terms/concepts overlap with faith and help to refine and fill out our understanding of what it means to respond to the gospel.

Faith

The debate over the meaning of *faith* revolves around whether faith not only includes belief and trust but also, in some form, obedience and faithfulness. Sometimes the discussion is driven by a concern that, if faith is just receiving the free gift of salvation, then this lowers or even removes the expectation that those who are justified are to live lives pleasing to God. It is true that Paul can use *pistis* to mean

12 Moo, *A Theology of Paul and His Letters*, 521.

"faithful" (e.g., 3:3) and *pisteuō* to mean "entrust" (e.g., 3:2). And the Old Testament can use "faith" language—the noun *ʾemunah* and the verb *ʾaman*—with the sense of "faithfulness" and "trustworthiness."[13] The evidence, however, favors taking faith as a response to the gospel.

Faith is not something a person does but is "fundamentally receptive."[14] Those who respond positively to the gospel "receive [*lambanontes*] the abundance of grace and the free gift of righteousness" (5:17; see more on this text below). In Romans saving faith is contrasted with works and, in such contexts, consists of belief and trust. Faith is trusting the promises of God (4:20). As Douglas Moo points out, in many Old Testament passages "the language of 'believing' refers to a fundamental attitude of trust in and dependence on God—a meaning that is quite close to the typical Pauline use of *pist-* language."[15] This emphasis on faith as trust in Christ is clear in 1:16–17. Roy Ciampa argues in connection with Paul's quotation of Habakkuk 2:4 in Romans 1:17 that Paul uses the phrase "by faith" (*ek pisteōs*) repeatedly (see Rom. 3:26; 4:16; 5:1; 9:30, 32; 10:6; 14:23) "as a snippet quotation of Habakkuk 2:4"[16] to describe those who are justified by faith.

It is not that Paul is unconcerned about the moral renewal of those who come to faith. After all, he calls out the potential abuse of grace: "What shall we say then? Are we to continue in sin that grace may abound?" (Rom. 6:1). His answer in 6:1–23, however, is not to conflate faith and obedience but rather to insist that those who believe are united to Christ in his death and resurrection and live "under grace" (6:14). They are to present themselves "to God as those who have been

13 Moo, *A Theology of Paul and His Letters*, 524.

14 Thomas R. Schreiner, *Paul, Apostle of God's Glory in Christ: A Pauline Theology*, 2nd ed. (Downers Grove, IL: IVP Academic, 2020), 248.

15 Moo, *A Theology of Paul and His Letters*, 525–26. Cf. Ex. 14:31; Deut. 1:32; Ps. 78:37; Isa. 7:9; 28:16; 43:10; Jonah 3:5.

16 Roy E. Ciampa, "Old Testament in Paul," in *DPL*² 725. For the details see Roy E. Ciampa, "Habakkuk 2:4 in Romans: Echoes, Allusions, and Rewriting," in *Scripture, Texts, and Tracings in Romans*, ed. A. Das and L. Belleville (Philadelphia: Fortress Academic, 2021), 11–29.

brought from death to life" (6:13). In systematic theology terms, Paul sees justification and sanctification as inseparable but distinct phases of salvation by grace.

Repentance

Often paired with *faith* as the desired response to the gospel, *repentance* appears infrequently in Romans. God's kindness is meant to lead people to "repentance" (*metanoia*, Rom. 2:4), a remorseful change of mind, a turning away from sin and toward God. As Paul says elsewhere, "Godly grief produces a repentance that leads to salvation" (2 Cor. 7:10). Paul reports the reception his gospel received among the Thessalonians: They "turned to God from idols to serve the living and true God" (1 Thess. 1:9). The concept of repentance is implied in Romans 6 and 8 where Paul speaks of denying the flesh and becoming slaves of righteousness.

Confessing That Jesus Is Lord

In Romans 10:9–10, faith is paired with confession as the human response to the gospel of salvation and justification: "If you *confess* with your mouth that Jesus is Lord and *believe* in your heart that God raised him from the dead, you will be saved. For with the heart one believes and is justified, and with the mouth one *confesses* and is saved." Confession here goes beyond a mere assent to the truth of something; it is an acknowledgement of the lordship of the risen Christ, a verbal and public profession of allegiance.

Calling on the Name of the Lord

Three times in Romans 10:12–14, Paul describes responding to the gospel as "calling on the name of the Lord" in association with faith/believing: "For there is no distinction between Jew and Greek; for the same Lord is Lord of all, bestowing his riches on *all who call on him*. For '*everyone who calls on the name of the Lord* will be saved.' How then will *they call on him* in whom they have not *believed*?" Calling on the name of the Lord results in salvation in Romans 10:13 and is paired with believing in the Lord in 10:14. Paul cites Joel 2:32 (Joel 3:5 LXX), where "Lord" refers to Yahweh. But in the context of Romans 10 "Lord" refers to Jesus. Strikingly, "Paul ascribes the same status to Jesus as Joel ascribes to God"[17] (a point to which we shall return in chapter 7). Calling on the name of the Lord Jesus is the equivalent of confessing him as the only true God, the only one worthy of our worship and allegiance. One way of referring to Christians is "those who call on the name of the Lord" (see Acts 9:14, 21; 22:16; 1 Cor. 1:2; 2 Tim. 2:22). Like faith, it is an initial response to the gospel that continues as a customary action when believers address God in prayer and acclaim him in their meetings.

Receiving God's Grace and Gift

Paul points to the generosity and undeserved nature of the gift of salvation when he contrasts the careers and legacies of Adam and Christ (Rom. 5:15–17). Here "righteousness is not earned but bestowed; those who are in Christ should live righteously, but because of God's gift rather than in order to achieve it."[18] Significantly for our purposes, Paul describes those who respond in faith as "those who receive . . . the free gift of righteousness" (5:17). As a synonym for faith, the verb "to receive" offers clear support for the view that responding to the gospel is a matter of believing trust and resting rather than a matter of active doing and working.

Putting One's Hope in the Messiah

In Romans 15:9–12 Paul cites four Old Testament passages (Ps. 18:49; Deut. 32:43; Ps. 117:1; Isa. 11:10, respectively), all of which refer to "the Gentiles," stressing "Paul's own understanding of both the Christian gospel and his God-given Gentile mission."[19] The fourth passage,

17 Robert W. Yarbrough, *Romans*, in *Romans–Galatians*, vol. 10 of *ESV Expository Commentary*, ed. Iain M. Duguid, James M. Hamilton Jr., and Jay Sklar (Wheaton, IL: Crossway, 2020), 158.

18 Craig S. Keener, *Romans: A New Covenant Commentary* (Eugene, OR: Cascade, 2009), 76.

19 Richard N. Longenecker, *The Epistle to the Romans*, NIGTC (Grand Rapids, MI: Eerdmans, 2016), 1015.

Isaiah 11:10, mentions the Messiah's rule over Gentiles and the prophecy that "in him will the Gentiles hope" (Rom. 15:12). As a response to the gospel, once again, hope speaks of trust, a looking forward in confident expectation.

Baptism

Paul insists on "the incompatibility between baptism into Christ and remaining in sin."[20] He points to the significance of the baptism of the Roman Christians to make his point: "Do you not know that all of us who have been baptized into Christ Jesus were baptized into his death? We were buried therefore with him by baptism into death, in order that, just as Christ was raised from the dead by the glory of the Father, we too might walk in newness of life" (6:3–4).

It is unnecessary to see the sacrament of water baptism as either a component of responding to the gospel or a baptism into Christ. One signifies the other. "Baptism is the onetime sacrament of our immersion into Christ—literally the incorporation of our bodies into his body, or our selves into his very self."[21] In Romans 6, specifically, it is Christ's death to sin and rising to new life to which Paul points as the basis for our progressive "sanctification" (6:22). Paul is not saying that baptism in and of itself has the power to save; water baptism seals, for those baptised as believers, the experience of putting one's faith in Christ. As such, like confessing the lordship of Christ (see above), it shows that saving faith is not a private or passive thing; believing trust leads to a public action underscoring the change that salvation brings.

Conclusion

Salvation is by grace through faith. In this chapter, we have clarified and filled out this gospel summary, confirming its twin emphases—grace and faith. We are indeed saved by the amazing grace of God, which is

20 Michael F. Bird, *Romans*, SGBC 6 (Grand Rapids, MI: Zondervan Academic, 2016), 196.

21 Kevin P. Emmert, *The Water and the Blood: How the Sacraments Shape Christian Identity* (Wheaton: IL: Crossway, 2023), 102. Cf. "clothed with Christ" (Gal. 3:27 CSB).

superabundant, antecedent, incongruous, and efficacious. We respond in faith—that is, repenting of our sins, confessing Jesus as Lord, calling on his name, receiving God's gracious gift with thanksgiving, putting our hope in the Messiah, and being baptized.

6

The Gospel and the Old Testament

The Law and the Prophets bear witness.

ROMANS 3:21

PAUL'S USE OF THE OLD TESTAMENT, "the Scriptures" or "Scripture" in Paul's parlance, is a critical topic in Romans.[1] If "the gospel of God" is the theme of the letter, Paul declares that the gospel was "promised beforehand through his prophets in the holy Scriptures" (1:2). Romans contains more than half of the Old Testament quotations in Paul's letters, 59 out of 117 according to one count,[2] and many passages in Romans are effectively commentary on Old Testament texts.[3]

1 Aaron Sherwood, *Romans: A Structural, Thematic, and Exegetical Commentary* (Bellingham, WA: Lexham, 2020), 67: "Next to structure and occasion, attending to Paul's use of Scripture in Romans is the most important control in soundly interpreting Romans."

2 Cf. the list in Roy E. Ciampa, "The Old Testament in Paul," in *DPL*[2] 726–29. The Old Testament quotations are concentrated in four main sections of the letter: 2:1–3:20; 4:1–8; 9:1–11:36; and 15:7–13.

3 E.g., Paul comments on Gen. 15:6 and Ps. 32 in Rom. 4:1–25. And in Rom. 10:1–21, he comments on Lev. 18:5; Deut. 9:4; 30:12–14; Isa. 28:16; Joel 2:32; Isa. 52:7; Nah. 1:15; Isa. 53:1; Ps. 19:4; Deut. 32:21; Isa. 65:1–2, respectively. Paul expounds his doctrine of justification by faith with reference to three key texts from Scripture: (1) Hab. 2:4 in Rom. 1:17 (with echoes of "by faith" in 3:26, 30; 5:1; 9:30, 32); (2) Gen. 15:6 in Rom. 4:3, 9, 22; and (3) Lev. 18:5 in Rom. 10:5. Ciampa, "The Old Testament in Paul," 726–28, notes that Hab. 2:4 is also cited in Gal. 3:9, 11 (with echoes of "by faith" in Gal. 2:16; 3:7, 8, 22, 24; 5:5) and Lev. 18:5 is cited in Gal. 3:12.

However, attending only to explicit references to the Old Testament is a titanic exegetical mistake, for the quotations are only the tip of the iceberg of scriptural influence. Throughout Romans there are numerous Old Testament allusions and echoes, along with references to Old Testament concepts (e.g., judgment, salvation, peace, Messiah, election, etc.) and figures (e.g., Abraham, David, Adam, Jacob, Esau, Pharaoh).

Paul's use of the Old Testament in Romans has deep roots and many branches. David Peterson offers a good summary:

> Paul uses Scripture in this letter *didactically* in relation to God's character, his covenantal commitment to Abraham and his offspring, and the saving message of the gospel. He interprets it *prophetically* in relation to the Messiah, Israel, and the nations. . . . He employs it in a *hortatory* way, to encourage Christians to make appropriate responses to God and his will, *missiologically* to explain his own ministry and agenda, and *doxologically* to encourage celebration of God's saving achievement through his Son.[4]

The use of Scripture in Romans is not another volume in the Romans theological encyclopedia as much as the shelf on which all the other volumes sit. For that reason, Paul's use of Scripture appears in every chapter of this book. In this chapter, instead of attempting a comprehensive survey, which would take too much space and overlap with other topics, I will focus on two matters that are critical for understanding Romans: Scripture as prophecy of the gospel and the complicated question of the law in Romans.

The Old Testament as Prophecy of the Gospel

There are five statements in Romans that express Paul's belief that the Old Testament Scriptures point to salvation in Christ:

1. "The gospel of God" was "promised beforehand through his prophets in the Holy Scriptures" (1:1–2).

4 David G. Peterson, "The Letter to the Romans," in *DNTUOT* 716.

2. The disclosure of "the righteousness of God" is attested by "the Law and the Prophets" (3:21).
3. We "uphold the law" as prophecy in stressing the critical role of faith in justifying both Jews and Gentiles (3:31).
4. The account of Abraham's faith being "counted to him as righteousness" was written for believers in Christ (4:22–24).
5. "The revelation of the mystery," which is the gospel about Jesus Christ, is disclosed through the "prophetic writings," which includes the law (16:25–26).

The first and final texts, which envelop the letter, supply precedent for labelling this section as "The Old Testament as Prophecy of the Gospel," given their use of the noun "prophets" (1:2) and the adjective "prophetic" (16:26). In 1:2 Paul affirms that the gospel was promised in advance in the Holy Scriptures "through his prophets" (*dia tōn prophētōn autou*); in 16:26 this gospel is disclosed "through the prophetic writings [or "Scriptures"]" (*dia . . . graphōn prophētikōn*).

Romans 3:21 is the programmatic text for Paul's use of the Old Testament as prophecy of the gospel: There Paul declares that "the Law and the Prophets bear witness" to the saving righteousness of God. As C. E. B. Cranfield notes, this "attestation of the gospel by the OT is of fundamental importance for Paul [which] is indicated by the solemn way in which he insists on it here in what is one of the great hinge sentences on which the argument of the epistle turns."[5] Indeed, along with its tone and placement, the uncommon language it uses underlines its significance: Paul nowhere else in his letters uses the phrase, "the Law and the Prophets," and this is the only time Paul uses the verb *martureō* in reference to the witness of Scripture.[6]

5 C. E. B. Cranfield, *A Critical and Exegetical Commentary on the Epistle to the Romans: Introduction and Commentary on Romans 1–8*, ICC (Edinburgh: T&T Clark, 1975), 203.

6 The imagery of the law court in the background of 1:18–3:18 and to the fore in 3:19–20 explains the use of "testimony" language (*martureō*); the law and the prophets are summoned as witnesses to "the righteousness of God through faith in Jesus Christ for all who believe" (3:22).

But to what in particular do the Law and the Prophets testify? Most commentators, if they answer this question, do so in general ways with little attempt at validating their opinion from the rest of Romans. Joseph Fitzmyer and James Dunn are exceptions. Fitzmyer suggests that Romans 4:23–24 "illustrate" the Old Testament bearing witness to the gospel.[7] Dunn points in the same direction to the rest of the epistle: "The testimony he will subsequently elaborate, particularly in chaps. 4 and 9–11, is of a community in the character of God's saving purpose through Israel."[8]

As it turns out, in Romans Paul cites the Law (i.e., the Pentateuch) in tandem with the Prophets as a prophecy of the gospel on six occassions:

- In Romans 4 the Law and the Prophets testify to righteousness by faith apart from the law: in connection with Abraham's faith in Genesis 15:6, 22 (Rom. 4:1–4, 9–25) and David's forgiveness in Psalm 32:1–2 (Rom. 4:6–8).
- In Romans 9 the Law and the Prophets testify to the partial hardening of Israel that has accompanied the gospel: in Genesis 21:12; 18:10, 14; 25:23; Exodus 33:19; 9:16 (Rom. 9:6–18) and in Malachi 1:2–3; Isaiah 29:16; 45:9; 10:22–23; 1:9; Hosea 2:23; 1:10 (Rom. 9:25–29).[9]
- In Romans 10 the Law and the Prophets testify to righteousness by faith: in Deuteronomy 9:4; 30:11–14 (Rom. 10:6–9) and in Isaiah 28:16; 53:1; Joel 2:32 (Rom. 10:11–15).
- In Romans 10 the Law and the Prophets testify to not all Israelites accepting the gospel: in Deuteronomy 32:21 (Rom. 10:19) and in Psalm 19:4; Isaiah 65:1–2 (Rom. 10:18, 20–21).
- In Romans 11 the Law and the Prophets testify to the hardening of Israel: "as it is written" in Deuteronomy 29:4; Isaiah 29:10 (Rom. 11:8) and "and David says" in Psalm 69:22–23 (Rom. 11:9–10).

7 Joseph A. Fitzmyer, *Romans: A New Translation with Introduction and Commentary*, AB 33 (New York: Doubleday, 1993), 344.

8 James D. G. Dunn, *Romans 1–8*, WBC (Dallas: Word, 1988), 166.

9 Cf. Mark A. Seifrid, "Romans," in *CNTUOT* 639: "The law itself defines the children of Abraham and of Israel as those created by the word of promise."

- In Romans 15 the Law and the Prophets testify to Gentiles glorifying God: in Deuteronomy 32:43; 2 Samuel 22:50; Psalm 18:49; Psalm 117:1; Isaiah 11:10 (Rom. 15:9–12).

The issue of Jews and Gentiles in the people of God is a recurring theme in Paul's rendition of the testimony of the Law and Prophets to the gospel in Romans. However, it would be unwise to conclude that according to Paul the witness of the prophetic Scriptures is limited to or even focused on this question. Paul tends to cite Scripture explicitly more often when dealing with questions with which his Jewish readers and opponents took issue. The concentration of quotations in Romans 9–11 that deals with the election of Israel and the inclusion of the Gentiles bears this out.[10]

Note, too, that in citing the Law and the Prophets as testimony to the gospel in the six examples above Paul has chosen to cite texts drawn first from the Law and then from the Prophets, a clearly discernible sequence. The only partial exception is the quotation of Psalm 19:4 in Romans 10:18, which is followed by a quotation from Deuteronomy and then Isaiah. I am not suggesting that this pattern of citing the Law and then the Prophets is contrived or even conscious on Paul's part. However, it is striking that the only place in his letters where he refers to Scripture as "the Law and the Prophets" is in Romans 3:21, which sets up his repeated appeal to the Law and the Prophets as a witness to the gospel in the rest of the letter.

The Law in Romans

The word "law," *nomos,* occurs more often in Romans than in the rest of Paul's letters combined (seventy-four versus forty-seven times). Indeed, the law of Moses is a central topic in the theology of the letter and

10 According to UBS^4, there are sixty-two Old Testament quotations in Romans, with thirty-two in Rom. 9–11. In fact, up to a third of all of the quotations of Scripture in all of Paul's letters, depending on how you count them, occur in Rom. 9–11. Cf. Seifrid, "Romans." *CNTUOT* 638: "The long drought of direct citation of the Scriptures in chapters 5–8, which Paul breaks in 8:36, is followed by a flood of citations in chapters 9–11."

plays a vital role in Paul's understanding of the gospel, judgment, the relationship between Jews and Gentiles, and his teaching on Christian living. Unfortunately, the law is also a confusing subject for many readers. Paul seems to say conflicting things about the law, describing it, on the one hand, as "holy and righteous and good" (7:12) and a positive gift of God (9:4) and, on the other hand, as an enslaving power that increases trespasses and brings about death through sin (5:20; 7:5). But the coherence of Paul's teaching about the law in Romans can be seen when we distinguish the various functions of the law.[11]

Paul rejects the law as law-covenant and legal code. Leviticus 18:5 states that the law was meant to lead to life. But according to Romans 10:5, which quotes this text, the law is a failed path to life and, as a result of sin, leads to death. It is not just that the law is obsolete and a new phase of salvation history has arrived. Nor is it that the law marked off the Jewish people and not the new people of God, which now includes Gentile believers too. Sprinkle is right that "whatever Paul found wrong with the law is contained *in nuce* in his understanding of Lev 18:5."[12] "Paul understands the Leviticus formula to be a summary of the law."[13] For Paul, the essence of the law as law-covenant or legal code is its call for something to be done in order to find life. Yet he sees that this path has failed, due to the universal sinfulness of humanity; instead, the law has led to death. As Westerholm observes, "Paul regards the mark of the old covenant as its demand for obedience and sees the reason for its failure in human transgressions."[14] Hence it is no surprise that Paul says that the alternative to being under the law is to be under grace (Rom. 6:14–15). Believers in Christ "stand in grace" (cf. 5:2). As Westerholm puts it, "Paul believes the coming of the new covenant implies the inadequacy of the old. . . . He characterizes the one as resting on divine

11 See Brian S. Rosner, *Paul and the Law: Keeping the Commandments of God,* NSBT (Downers Grove, IL: IVP Academic, 2013).

12 Preston M. Sprinkle, *Law and Life: The Interpretation of Leviticus 18:5 in Early Judaism and in Paul,* WUNT 2/241(Tübingen: Mohr Siebeck, 2008), 1.

13 Sprinkle, *Law and Life,* 193.

14 Stephen Westerholm, *Israel's Law and the Church's Faith: Paul and His Recent Interpreters* (Grand Rapids, MI: Eerdmans, 1988), 165.

grace, the other on human works."[15] Believers in Christ are not under the dominion of the law (6:14–15; 7:1–6).

However, in Romans, even though there is a sense in which all believers—both Jewish and Gentile—are not under the law, there is also a more limited sense in which Jewish believers may choose to live under the law. This more limited sense is clearly demonstrated in 14:1–15:6, a passage in which Paul addresses the observance or nonobservance of certain laws from the law of Moses in the Roman churches (see chapter 12 below). On such matters, Paul teaches that each individual is to act in accordance with his own convictions (14:5–6). As he states in 14:22, "The faith that you have, keep to yourself before God" (my translation). In effect, Paul allows for the expression of Jewish cultural tradition, living under the law's direction but not its dominion.

That Christians do not relate to the law as a legal code is clear when we look at how Paul describes Jews in relation to the law in 2:17–29. There Paul explains that Jews

- rely on the law;
- boast about the law;
- know God's will through the law;
- are educated in the law;
- have light, knowledge, and truth because of the law;
- do, observe, and keep the law;
- on occasion transgress the law;
- possess the law as a letter, written code, book, decrees, or commandments.

Remarkably, Paul never says in Romans or in any of his letters that believers in Christ relate to the law in any of these ways.[16] Rather, Paul says that "the righteous requirement of the law [is] fulfilled in us" (8:4).

15 Westerholm, *Israel's Law and the Church's Faith*, 163.

16 See Brian S. Rosner, "Paul and the Law: What He Did Not Say," *JSNT* 32, no. 4 (2010): 405–19.

Two other functions of the law are clearly taught in Romans, underscoring the ongoing validity of the law under the new covenant. First, as explained in the first half of this chapter, the law, along with the prophets, is a witness to the gospel. Second, the law functions for all Christians as wisdom for living. The remainder of the chapter will consider this latter function.

Paul states, "Whatever was written in former days [i.e., the Old Testament] was written for our [ethical] instruction [*eis tēn hēmeteran didaskalian*]" (Rom. 15:4). In at least three places in Romans, Paul quotes the law in relation to Christian living: not retaliating against enemies (Deut. 32:35 in Rom. 12:19–20); loving other Christians as the fundamental obligation (Ex. 20:13–17 / Deut. 5:17–21; Lev. 19:18 in Rom. 13:9); and welcoming one another (Deut. 32:43 in Rom. 15:9–12; cf. 14:1). However, the influence of the law on Paul's ethical teaching goes far beyond explicit citations. Reading the law as wisdom for Paul means that he internalizes the law and undertakes reflective and expansive applications based in part on the moral order of creation and the character of God that stand behind the law.

The influence of the commandment against murder (Ex. 20:13; Deut. 5:17) on Paul's moral teaching in Romans is a revealing example of reading the law in this way.[17] Romans refers to the commandment not to murder on two occasions (Rom. 1:29; 13:9). But a full appreciation of the influence of the murder commandment in Paul's moral teaching requires some attention to contemporary Jewish use of the commandment, along with the use of the commandment in the Old Testament. In brief, murder was widely regarded as the quintessential antisocial sin, the opposite of love. Other laws overlapped with murder, and the notion of murder was exploited in its capacity as a metaphor for social injustice including anger and malicious speech.

Paul's extensive use of other expressions for murder-related activity in Romans is also significant. He quotes Scripture on murderous

17 See William A. Williamson, "The Influence of 'You Shall Not Murder' on Paul's Ethics in Romans and 1 Corinthians" (PhD thesis, University of Western Sydney / Moore College, 2007), which these final two paragraphs summarize and build upon.

speech ("The venom of asps is under their lips") and murderous deeds ("Their feet are swift to shed blood") (3:13–15). He personifies sin and depicts it as a killer in his discussion of sin and the law (7:11). Paul also refers to being killed and persecuted for God's sake (8:35–36). Elijah is quoted as pleading to God against Israel: "Lord, they have killed your prophets, . . . and they seek my life" (11:3). Paul speaks of those who persecute God's people (12:14, 17–21). Finally, he warns the strong about destroying those who are weak in faith (14:13, 15, 20, 21). Thus, the influence of the murder commandment in Romans is pervasive, in spite of the fact that Paul nowhere says or implies that believers are under the law.

Conclusion

Paul's gospel did not come out of the blue but, rather, has deep roots in the Jewish Scriptures. The gospel only makes sense when we pay close attention to the fact that it was "promised beforehand through his prophets in the holy Scriptures" (1:2). The rich backstory of the gospel gives it depth and color, rendering it more winsome and compelling. This is nowhere more evident than when we consider the person and work of Jesus Christ, a topic we turn to next.

7

The Person and Work of Christ

Christ died for the ungodly.

ROMANS 5:6

FROM THE VERY BEGINNING of Romans, we learn that the central figure in the gospel is Jesus Christ. Paul writes that he was "set apart for the gospel of God" (1:1), which is a message "concerning his [God's] Son" (1:3). In Romans 1:3–4, Paul presents "a brief but poignant summary of the gospel"[1] containing "two important claims about the Son, leading to the climactic declaration that the Son is 'Jesus Christ our Lord'":[2]

> Concerning God's Son:
> 1. who was descended from David according to the flesh
> 2. was appointed the powerful Son of God according to the Spirit of holiness by the resurrection of the dead
>
> Jesus Christ our Lord.[3]

1 Michael J. Gorman, *Romans: A Theological and Pastoral Commentary* (Grand Rapids, MI: Eerdmans, 2022), 63.

2 David G. Peterson, *Commentary on Romans*, BTCP (Nashville: Holman Reference, 2017), 85.

3 This is my translation set out to highlight the structure of the passage.

The two claims speak of Jesus in terms of his human nature—he is the messianic Son of God in the line of King David—and in terms of his risen life—he is the exalted and ruling Son of God. As Peter Stuhlmacher notes, 1:3–4 "contain the history of Christ told in the Gospels in short form, and emphasise that the entire way of Jesus, from his birth to his exaltation stands under the sign of the promises of God,"[4] that is, "promised beforehand through his prophets in the holy Scriptures" (1:2). Behind the two assertions in 1:3–4 stand God's promises that a descendant of David would reign on his throne forever (2 Sam. 7:12–16)[5] and that the Lord would appoint David's Lord to the place of sovereign rule (Ps. 110:1). Every element in this elegant gospel precis is significant. Indeed, many passages in the letter hark back to it. In particular, the climactic declaration that God's Son is "Jesus Christ our Lord" is the refrain of Romans, reappearing "in different forms at significant points in the rest of the letter (Rom. 5:11, 21; 6:23; 7:25; 8:39; 13:14; 15:6)."[6]

In this chapter, we consider what Romans teaches about the person and work of Jesus Christ. As we will see, the two are closely related. The identity of Jesus is closely aligned with his work.

The Person of Christ

Looking at what Jesus is called in Romans is a good place to start our investigation of Christology in the letter. Nine names and titles call for our attention: Jesus, Christ/Messiah, Lord, Son or Son of God, the deliverer, the stone of stumbling and rock of offense, the last Adam, servant to the circumcised, and (the most startling) God over all. Some of these have a long backstory in the Old Testament and early Judaism and even appear in Romans in quotations from Scripture. Indeed, many could have the adjective "long-awaited" added as a prefix. The first four are the most important for Romans and are given prominence in the programmatic gospel summary in 1:3–4.

4 Peter Stuhlmacher, *Paul's Letter to the Romans: A Commentary* (Edinburgh: T&T Clark, 1994), 19.

5 Cf. Isa. 9:6–7; 11:1–10; Jer. 23:5–6; Ezek. 34:23–24; Zech. 9:9–10; 12:7–13:1.

6 Peterson, *Commentary on Romans*, 231.

Jesus

The name Jesus appears thirty-six times in Romans, often in combinations with other names and titles.[7] The Greek form of the Hebrew name *Joshua*, *Jesus* has the meaning "savior" or "the Lord is salvation." While it would be unwise to attach too much significance to its etymology, Jesus's name is connected to his mission: Joseph was told by the angel of the Lord that Mary "will bear a son, and you shall call his name *Jesus*, for he will *save his people from their sins*" (Matt. 1:21). In Romans the name fits well with his central role in the gospel of salvation. For example, Jesus's death saves us from the wrath of God (Rom. 5:9), we are saved by Jesus's risen life (5:10), and we are saved when we confess that Jesus is Lord (10:9).

Christ/Messiah

Christos occurs sixty-five times in Romans, most often in combinations with "Jesus" or "the Lord." The Greek noun is related to the Greek and Hebrew verbs for "to smear" and came to mean "anointed" or "consecrated" in the sense of being singled out or chosen. In the Old Testament, prophets, priests, and kings were anointed. The seeds of a coming messianic Davidic king are planted in the Old Testament and grew stronger in some quarters of early Judaism:

- "The kings of the earth set themelves . . . / against the LORD and against his Anointed" (Ps. 2:2)
- "The coming of an anointed one, a prince" (Dan. 9:25)
- "Their king shall be the Lord Messiah" (Ps. Sol. 17:32 OTP)
- "The appointed day when his Messiah will reign" (Ps. Sol. 18:5 OTP)

Scholars debate whether *Christos* in Paul's letters, given its ubiquity (212x), retains a titular sense or is simply a name for Jesus. Most modern English versions usually translate it as "Christ," with a few using "Messiah" in contexts where the sense of a coming Davidic king is to the fore. Michael Bird's conclusion fits well in the case of Romans:

7 E.g., "Jesus Christ" occurs seventeen times in the letter.

"Even if *Christos* functions as a proper name for Jesus in Paul's letters, there are clear indications that the royal-messianic connotations were maintained."[8] In Romans, *Christos* is connected with Jesus's Davidic descent in 1:3 and in 15:12:

> The root of Jesse will come,
> even he who arises to rule the Gentiles. (quoting Isa. 11:10)

The Jewish expectation of a coming King is also clear in Romans 9:5: "Theirs are the patriarchs, and from them is traced the human ancestry of the Messiah [*Christos*]" (NIV). As Douglas Moo states, "Calling Jesus 'Christ' serves to remind early Christians, whether Jewish or gentile, that he is the fulfilment of the Old Testament expectation about an eschatological redeemer."[9]

Lord

The word "lord" (*kyrios*) is occasionally used in the mundane sense of a human "lord" or "master" in the LXX and New Testament (e.g., Gen. 31:35; Matt. 25:11 [CSB]; Rom. 14:4). It also refers to God over six thousand times in the LXX, translating both *Yahweh* (the tetragrammaton or personal name of God rendered as "Lord" in the ESV) and *adonai*. In the Greco-Roman world, *kyrios* was used of secular rulers such as the Roman emperor (as was "Son of God"; see below). Paul uses *kyrios* in Romans forty-three times—around thirty-three for Jesus and ten for God the Father.[10] Paul indicates that Jesus was installed as Lord at his resurrection (Rom. 1:3; cf. 4:24: "Believe in him who raised from the dead Jesus our Lord"), and he makes confession of Jesus as the risen Lord the essence of Christian belief: "If you confess with your mouth that Jesus is Lord and believe in your heart that God raised him from the dead, you will be saved" (10:9).

8 Michael Bird, "Christology," in *DPL*^{2} 101.

9 Douglas J. Moo, *A Theology of Paul and His Letters: The Gift of the New Realm in Christ*, BTNT (Grand Rapids, MI: Zondervan Academic, 2021), 366.

10 Some of the referents of *kyrios* in Romans (and in Paul's other letters) are debated.

Two points about the lordship of Christ stand out in Romans. First, all believers live under the authority of Jesus as the risen Lord. This is especially clear when Paul insists that in disputable matters believers answer directly to the Lord Jesus:

> Who are you to pass judgment on the servant of another? It is before his own master [*kyrios*] that he stands or falls. . . . If we live, we live to the Lord [*kyrios*], and if we die, we die to the Lord [*kyrios*]. So then, whether we live or whether we die, we are the Lord's [*kyrios*]. For to this end Christ died and lived again, that he might be Lord [*kyrios*] both of the dead and of the living. (14:4, 8–9)

As the risen Lord, Jesus Christ is worthy of our obedience and worship.

Second, when Paul calls Jesus Christ "Lord" in several texts in Romans, it implies that he is God. In the culmination of a discussion (Rom. 10:9–12), Paul quotes Joel 2:32—"Everyone who calls on the name of the Lord will be saved" (Rom. 10:13). Although the prophet was originally referring to the Lord God, Paul clearly applies "Lord" to Jesus Christ. Several other Old Testament texts about God are possibly applied to Jesus in Romans (see Isa. 10:22–23 in Rom. 9:27–28; Isa. 1:9 in Rom. 9:29; Isa. 52:7 in Rom. 10:16; 1 Kings 19:10, 14 in Rom. 11:3; Isa. 59:20 in Rom. 11:25–26; Isa. 45:23 in Rom. 14:11; Ps. 117:1 in Rom. 15:11).[11] It is not that Paul thinks of Jesus as the totality of Israel's God. He still distinguishes between God the Father and the Lord Jesus (1:7), and he sees glory being directed to God through Jesus Christ (16:27). That Romans affirms the divine status of Jesus, "relationally distinct from but organic to God the Father,"[12] is confirmed in the doxology of 9:5 (see below).

Son of God

Compared with Jesus, Christ/Messiah, and Lord, the title "Son of God" occurs less frequently in Romans (six times as "his [God's] Son" and

11 See Larry W. Hurtado, *Lord Jesus Christ: Devotion to Jesus in Earliest Christianity* (Grand Rapids, MI: Eerdmans, 2005), 108–18.

12 Bird, "Christology," 102.

once as "Son of God"), and it is not used exclusively for Jesus, for it also describes believers. However, this relative paucity and nonexclusive application belies the title's importance, given its occurrence at critical junctures and its foundational support for several major doctrines.

As the descendant of David, Jesus is the Son of God, destined to rule forever as prophesied in the Davidic covenant (2 Sam. 7:12–16; cf. Pss. 2:7; 89:3–4, 19–37). However, Romans takes this royal identity a step further and stresses Jesus's divine sonship, describing him as the risen "powerful Son of God" (Rom. 1:4 CSB). In this sense, "Son of God" is not just a synonym for "Messiah." Jesus as the Son of God is the bringer of salvation: "We were reconciled to God by the death of his Son" (5:10; cf. 8:3, 32). He is God's "own Son" (8:3, 32), underscoring Jesus's uniquely close relationship to God the Father. That Jesus is sent by God (8:3) intimates his preexistence. As Larry Hurtado puts it, the title Son of God "primarily expresses Jesus's unique standing and intimate favor with God, and God's direct involvement in Jesus's redemptive work."[13]

The overlap of sonship language between Jesus and believers—"All who are led by the Spirit of God are sons of God" (8:14)[14]—reveals another layer of meaning in "the gospel of his [God's] Son" (1:9). Both male and female believers are sons of God by virtue of our union with God's Son. We address God as "Abba! Father!" (8:15), and as "children of God" we are "fellow heirs with Christ" (8:16–17). We are part of God's family and heirs thanks to the Son of God. A foundational doctrine in

13 Hurtado, *Lord Jesus Christ,* 104.

14 That *huios* is generic in 8:14, including both male and female believers, is clear from 8:16–17 where Paul refers to believers as "children [*tekna*] of God." It is worth retaining "sons" in translating 8:14 (and Gal. 4:7) since the context concerns inheritance. In Bible times it was the right of the eldest son in the family to be the primary heir (cf. Num. 27:8; 36:1–12; Deut. 21:15–17). Julie Canlis, "The Fatherhood of God and Union with Christ in Calvin," in *"In Christ" in Paul: Explorations in Paul's Theology of Union and Participation*, ed. Michael J. Thate, Kevin J. Vanhoozer, and Constantine R. Campbell (Tübingen: Mohr Siebeck, 2014), 404: "I am unwilling to drop the gendered term 'sonship,' as our 'sonship' is founded upon Christ's own Sonship. For those who find the term suspect, I do not think it can be interchanged with all sorts of terms like 'becoming children of God' or 'being adopted,' . . . these lose christological clarity."

Romans, the sonship of Jesus "is filial, preexistent, Davidic, redemptive, eschatological, and participatory."[15]

Deliverer

In Romans 11:26–27, Paul quotes Isaiah 59:20–21 (a text to which we shall return in chapter 10 in connection with the salvation of "all Israel"). Paul's citation identifies Jesus Christ as "the Deliverer" (*ho rhyomenos*) who "will come from Zion" (Rom. 11:26). A deliverer is someone who comes to "save, rescue, deliver, preserve" someone from peril or danger.[16] The word overlaps in meaning with "Savior," a term Paul uses elsewhere both of Jesus (Eph. 5:23; Phil. 3:20; 2 Tim. 1:10; Titus 1:4; 2:13; 3:6) and God (1 Tim. 1:1; 2:3; 4:10; Titus 1:3; 2:10). As Mark Keown points out, "The mention of Zion [in 11:26] again asserts Jesus's Davidic and messianic credentials."[17] The deliverance that Jesus brings "will banish ungodliness" (Rom. 11:26; evoking the wrath of God in 1:18) and will pave the way for a new "covenant" to "take away their sins" (11:27).

Stone of Stumbling and a Rock of Offense

Paul explains the situation of unbelieving Jews. They pursued righteousness by works and not by faith which prompts God's judgment and an offer of salvation (Rom. 9:31–32). He cites a combination of Isaiah 28:16 and 8:14:

> Behold, I am laying in Zion a stone of stumbling, and a rock of
> offense [*skandalon*];
> and whoever believes in him will not be put to shame. (Rom. 9:33)

That Jesus is the stone/rock is clear from the invitation to "believe in him." The reference to Zion is another allusion to Jesus as the Davidic

15 Bird, "Christology," 103.

16 "Ῥύομαι," in BDAG 908. Paul uses the verb in 15:31 in his request for prayer to be delivered or kept safe from "the unbelievers in Judea."

17 Mark J. Keown, *Romans and the Mission of God* (Eugene, OR: Wipf and Stock, 2021), 86.

Messiah. Intriguingly, the Targum Isaiah 28:18 paraphrase also reads the text messianically: "I am about to appoint in Zion, a king, a strong king, powerful and terrible."[18] Whereas elsewhere in Paul's letters Jesus is the cornerstone of a new temple (Eph. 2:19–22), in Romans 9:32–33 he is the stone/rock that brings judgment (cf. 2:16) and salvation. The "offense" that Jews stumbled over is named in 1 Corinthians 1:23, where Paul writes, "We preach Christ crucified, a stumbling block [*skandalon*] to Jews and folly to Gentiles."

Last Adam

Paul compares Christ with Adam in Romans 5:12–21.[19] Whereas Adam's sin brought death to all those connected with him—a problem not solved by the giving of the law—Christ's life of obedience and sacrificial death brought righteousness, justification, and life to all those in union with him. Adam and Christ in this sense are epochal, representative, corporate figures, whose actions affect all those who belong to them. All human beings stand behind either the old Adam or the new Adam and are affected by their representative actions and their legacies. Elsewhere Paul states this message in brief: "As in Adam all die, so also in Christ shall all be made alive" (1 Cor. 15:22). However, Paul makes clear that the two groups are not coterminous: Reigning in life with Christ is restricted to "those who receive the abundance of grace and the free gift of righteousness" (Rom. 5:17). Believers are transferred from the realm of Adam to the realm of Christ. We will return to this passage below in connection with the representative nature of Christ's death.

Depicting Christ as "the eschatological counterpart of the primeval Adam"[20] reveals several things about the person of Christ. First, the idea of Christ and Adam as representative individuals provides the framework for Paul's argument that "our old self was crucified" with Christ, meaning our participation in the old era of Adam has been

18 Cited in Keown, *Romans and the Mission of God*, 86 (Keown's translation).

19 While Paul nowhere explicitly calls Jesus "the last Adam" in Romans, he calls Adam "a type of the one who was to come" (5:14).

20 Bird, "Christology," 103.

"brought to nothing" (6:6). Having died with Christ, we are "set free from [the power and dominion] of sin" (6:7). Second, Christ as the last Adam reminds us of his full humanity. God sent "his own Son in the likeness of sinful flesh and for sin" (8:3), meaning that the Son of God "assumes our human existence, assumes flesh, i.e., he exists in the state and position [of flesh], amid the conditions, under the curse and punishment of sinful man."[21] Finally, his being the fully human last Adam is the basis for describing the Son of God as the true image of God, a restoration of Adam's damaged image (8:29). As the last Adam, the Son of God is "the perfect divine image-bearer in his humanity."[22]

Servant to the Circumcised

Paul describes Christ as "a servant [*diakonos*] to the circumcised [the Jewish people]" (15:8), a title that points to his "divine commission to accomplish salvation."[23] Christ was sent by God "to show God's truthfulness" and faithfulness in confirming "the promises given to the patriarchs" (15:8), something Paul explains at length in Romans 9–11 (see chapter 10 below). A second aspect of Christ's assignment as God's servant was to extend "mercy" to the Gentiles (15:9). In fact this second purpose is related to the first since the Abrahamic covenant included blessing to all nations (see Gen. 12:3; 18:18; 22:18; 26:4).

God over All

In the discussion of the title "Lord" above, I noted that several Old Testament texts about the Lord God are quoted in Romans to describe the Lord Jesus Christ, most notably Joel 2:32 in Romans 10:13. But

21 Karl Barth, *Church Dogmatics,* ed. G. W. Bromiley and T. F. Torrance, 14 vols. (Edinburgh: T&T Clark, 1936), 2:155. Cited in Graham A. Cole, *The God Who Became Human: A Biblical Theology of Incarnation,* NSBT (Downers Grove, IL: IVP Academic, 2013), 142.

22 Gordon D. Fee, *Jesus the Lord according to Paul the Apostle: A Concise Introduction* (Grand Rapids, MI: Baker Academic, 2018), 113.

23 Thomas R. Schreiner, *Romans,* 2nd ed., BECNT (Grand Rapids, MI: Baker Academic, 2018), 728.

this is not the only way that the deity of Christ is taught in Romans. We may note two implicit affirmations and one explicit identification of Christ as God.

In the first implicit affirmation, Paul refers to "the Spirit of God" who indwells believers (8:9). As Charles L. Quarles notes, "In the very next sentence of the same verse this indwelling Spirit is referred to as the Spirit of Christ. By using 'God' and 'Christ' interchangeably, Paul strongly implies the deity of the Messiah."[24] Second, Paul closes his letter with a general greeting from "all the churches of Christ [*ekklēsiai tou Christou*]" (Rom. 16:16). Indeed, in 1 Corinthians 1:2 and 2 Corinthians 1:1, Paul describes the church in Corinth as "the church of God" (*ekklēsia tou theou*).

The clearest explicit ascription of divinity to Christ in the letter is the brief doxology of Romans 9:5: "To them [the Israelites] belong the patriarchs, and from their race, according to the flesh, is *the Christ, who is God over all*, blessed forever. Amen." Given that early Greek manuscripts did not have punctuation, some scholars prefer a translation that distinguishes Christ and God in this verse. For example, the RSV has a full stop instead of a comma after "Christ": "To them belong the patriarchs, and of their race, according to the flesh, is the Christ. *God who is over all* be blessed for ever. Amen." Though the debate continues, there are good reasons for preferring the identification of Christ as God, as the majority of English Bible translations do. In light of the implicit evidence mentioned above, it should not surprise us that "the Jesus of Romans is, in the very highest sense, Paul's Lord,"[25] even "God over all."

The Work of Christ

The death and resurrection of Christ are at the center of the gospel of God and have many dimensions. Both play multiple and complemen-

24 Charles L. Quarles, "Jesus' Identity in Romans," in *Paul's Letter to the Romans: Theological Essays*, ed. Douglas J. Moo, Eckhard J Schnabel, Thomas R. Schreiner, and Frank Thielman (Peabody, MA: Hendrikson Academic, 2023), 165.

25 Quarles, "Jesus' Identity in Romans," 168.

tary roles in securing and defining our salvation in Romans. In addition, while not a primary focus in Romans, the letter also has teaching on the significance of Christ's ascension and return. To set the scene, let's begin by noting Paul's remarkably comprehensive coverage in Romans of the key moments of the life of Christ.

The Life of Jesus Christ according to Romans

The teaching of Romans on both the person and work of Christ is set within an account of his life story. Intriguingly, many of the main points of the Apostles' Creed concerning God's Son are affirmed in Romans. While not a narrative of the life of the Son of God, Romans offers an outline of his story from his preexistence to his return:

Preexistence: God "[sent] his own Son" (8:3).

Earthly life: The "man Jesus Christ" (5:15) was "descended from David" (1:3) and "the patriarchs" (9:5), came "in the likeness of sinful flesh" (8:3), suffered (8:17), and was insulted by men (15:3).

Death: Jesus was "delivered up" (4:25), "crucified" (6:6), shed his blood (3:25), and "died to sin" (6:10) "for the ungodly" (5:6) and "for us" (5:8; cf. 8:33).

Burial: Jesus was buried (6:4).

Resurrection: "Jesus our Lord" was "raised from the dead" (4:24; cf. 1:4; 6:4; 8:34) so "that he might be Lord both of the dead and of the living" (14:9).

Ascension and exaltation: "Christ Jesus . . . is at the right hand of God . . . interceding for us" (8:34).

Return: "The day is at hand" (13:12) when "the Deliverer will come from Zion" (11:26) and "on that day . . . God [will judge] the secrets of men by Christ Jesus" (2:16).

The Death of Christ

In Romans, Jesus dies as our substitute, as our representative, in order to reveal God, and as an example of sacrificial love.

First, Jesus is our substitute. Two texts in Romans teach that Jesus bore God's judgment against our sins in our place to secure our forgiveness and our right standing before God. In 3:25 Paul explains that we are justified by grace because God put forward Christ Jesus as a *hilastērion*. This term is much discussed and has been variously translated as "propitiation," "expiation," "sacrifice of atonement," "place of atonement," and "mercy seat." Recently, the tide has been turning in favor of "mercy seat" or "place of atonement." Stephen Hultgren's two articles lay out the evidence convincingly:

> Biblical "atonement" is multifaceted, comprehending expiation and forgiveness, as well as removal of divine wrath. In the LXX the ἱλάσκομαι [*hilaskomai*] word group is also complex, retaining propitiatory overtones from classical usage (although it is often better to speak of God removing his own wrath), while taking on the additional meaning of expiation and forgiveness. The Pentateuchal ἱλαστήριον [*hilastērion*] is a "place" for such "atonement". Amidst many proposals, "the place of atonement" with allusion to the כַּפֹּרֶת [*kapōret*] remains the most likely meaning for ἱλαστήριον [*hilastērion*] in Rom. 3:25. Christ is the "place" where divine justice and mercy meet. His death is the visible manifestation of divine justice, the consequence of humanity's collective sin, which was "building up" towards a permanent breach in the relationship between God and humanity. Christ's death is also a ransom and the means by which God objectively removes sin and so frees humanity from death.[26]

Whereas Hultgren marginally favors "place of atonement" over "mercy seat" as the best English translation, I prefer "mercy seat," which is the most frequent meaning of the word in the LXX (twenty-one of twenty-six occurrences).[27] Sadly, most of the proposals for translating the word

26 Stephen Hultgren, "*Hilastērion* (Rom 3:25) and the Union of Divine Justice and Mercy. Part II: Atonement in the Old Testament and in Romans 1–5," *JTS* 70, no. 2 (2019): 546.

27 John D. Harvey, *Romans*, EGGNT (Nashville: B&H Academic, 2017), 93.

are obscure in English. "Propitiation" and "expiation" are not modern English, and "atonement" is also not in common usage. "Mercy seat" has the benefit of an established use in the Old Testament and is used in the ESV of Hebrews 9:5, the only other occurrence of the word in the New Testament.[28]

The mercy seat interpretation connects directly to the temple theme in Romans. Although Paul never explicitly rejects the Jewish temple, its priesthood, and its sacrifices, he implies as much in his use of cultic imagery to refer to the work of Christ. With respect to the temple theme in Romans, Paul identifies Christ as the mercy seat (Rom. 3:21–26), calls on believers to offer their bodies as living sacrifices (12:1–2), and characterizes his mission in terms of "priestly service" (15:16)—but not, it must be said, service in the Jerusalem temple.

The other text in Romans indicating that Jesus bore God's judgment against our sins in our place is 8:3. Paul states that those who are in Christ Jesus are not condemned before God, "for God has done what the law, weakened by the flesh, could not do. By sending his own Son in the likeness of sinful flesh and for sin, he condemned sin in the flesh, in order that the righteous requirement of the law might be fulfilled in us" (8:3–4). The phrase translated "for sin," *peri hamartias,* is an idiom for "sin offering" (see the NIV and CSB), which is how it is used in the LXX forty-four out of fifty-four times. We are set free from sin's condemnation by God's sending his Son as a sin offering, bearing our guilt and the wrath of God in our place. N. T. Wright comments correctly,

> No clearer statement is found in Paul, or indeed anywhere else in all Christian literature, of the early Christian belief that what happened on the cross was the judicial punishment of sin. . . . In Jesus' death

28 Cf. Frank S. Thielman, *Romans,* ZECNT (Grand Rapids, MI: Zondervan Academic, 2018), 754–55: "Jesus was the embodiment of the 'mercy seat' of Exodus 25:17–22 and Leviticus 16:2, 13–15. He was, then, the 'place' where God focused his presence among his people and where God atoned for their sins."

> the damnation that sin deserved was meted out fully and finally, so that sinners over whose heads that condemnation had hung might be liberated from this threat once and for all.[29]

Paul shows that the gospel was "promised beforehand . . . in the holy Scriptures" (Rom. 1:2). Our salvation was accomplished through the death of God's Son as a new mercy seat and a better sin offering, bearing God's judgment against our sins in our place. The sacrifice of God's Son also recalls Abraham offering his own son (Gen. 22:12–16), for in the ultimate act of love, God "did not spare his own Son but gave him up for us all" (Rom. 8:32).

Second, Jesus Christ not only dies in our place as our substitute but also dies as our representative, and we die with him. Union with Christ is arguably the central concept of both the means and blessings of salvation in Romans. The ground and source of many of the ideas of salvation is that believers are "in Christ." This is the case for redemption (3:24), freedom (8:2), eternal life (6:23), and holiness (6:2–3). In chapter 11, in the section "Dying and Rising with Christ," we look at the way in which our participation in Christ's death and resurrection enables us to end the reign of sin in our lives. Here, we focus on Paul's affirmation of the representative nature of the death and resurrection of Christ, which is expounded most directly in 6:3–4: "Do you not know that all of us who have been baptized into Christ Jesus were baptized into his death? We were buried therefore with him by baptism into death, in order that, just as Christ was raised from the dead by the glory of the Father, we too might walk in newness of life."

When we trust in Christ, his "story becomes our story, and our story is enfolded into his."[30] This can be seen when we compare Romans 6 with the outline of the story of Jesus Christ in the gospel summary of 1 Corinthians 15:1–9 (see table 7.1).[31]

29 N. T. Wright, "The Letter to the Romans," in *NIB* 10:574–75.

30 Michael J. Gorman, *Romans: A Theological and Pastoral Commentary* (Grand Rapids, MI: Eerdmans, 2022), 171.

31 Cf. Gorman, *Romans*, 170–71.

Table 7.1 Comparison of 1 Corinthians 15:1–9 and Romans 6:3–13

Event	1 Corinthians 15:1–9	Romans 6
Death	"Christ died" (15:3).	"All of us who have been baptized into Christ Jesus were baptized into his death" (6:3); "we have been united with him in a death like his" (6:5; cf. 6:6, 8, 11).
Burial	"He was buried" (15:4).	"We were buried therefore with him by baptism into death" (6:4).
Resurrection	"He was raised on the third day" (15:4).	"Just as Christ was raised from the dead . . . we too might walk in newness of life" (6:4); "we shall certainly be united with him in a resurrection like his" (6:5; cf. 6:8, 11).
Appearance / presentation	"He appeared to Cephas, then to the twelve," and to others (15:5–9) (In Acts 1:3 Jesus "presented [*paristēmi*] himself alive.")	"Present [*paristēmi*] yourselves to God as those who have been brought from death to life, and your members to God as instruments for righteousness" (6:13).

Third, the death of Jesus is a revelation of the character of God, displaying both his love and righteousness. Jesus's death shows that God is still perfectly righteous in declaring righteous those who put their faith in Jesus: "to show God's righteousness" (Rom. 3:25–26 [2x]). And Jesus's death also shows us God's extraordinary love: "God shows his love for us in that . . . Christ died for us" (5:8). Assertions about God's loving and righteous character are one thing, but the death of Jesus is a concrete demonstration and proof of his character that we can turn to with absolute confidence for all time. If we learn of God's existence and power from "the creation of the world" (1:20), the cross of Christ reveals two of God's central attributes in irrefutable and unforgettable terms.

Finally, the death of Jesus, along with his life, is an example of sacrificial love to be emulated by his followers (e.g., 15:1–3; this theme is explored in chapter 11).

The Resurrection of Christ

In Romans not only does Jesus rise from the dead as our representative (see discussion above) but also to reveal his true identity, confirm our justification, inaugurate the new creation, conquer evil, and give us new life.

First, the resurrection reveals Jesus's identity as "the powerful Son of God" (Rom. 1:4 CSB) and "Lord" (1:4). It was not as though his identity changed when he rose from the dead; he was already called the Son of God at his baptism (Mark 1:11).[32] Rather, the resurrection changed the status and appearance of Jesus Christ, from the meek and lowly Son of God to the supreme and powerful Son of God. If at the transfiguration we get a partial and temporary glimpse of the true and glorious identity of Jesus, at his resurrection that identity is permanently manifest. The gradual revelation of the identity of Jesus in the Gospels reaches its climax and is plainly and publicly displayed in the resurrection of Jesus for all to see. Similarly, the resurrection draws us into the reign of Jesus as the Lord of all: "To this end Christ died and lived again, that he might be Lord of both the dead and of the living" (Rom. 14:9).

Second, the resurrection of Jesus confirms our justification. "Jesus our Lord . . . was delivered up [by God] for our trespasses and raised [by God] for our justification" (Rom. 4:24–25). "In this verse there are strong echoes of Isaiah 53:5, 11–12, where Jesus appears as the Suffering Servant who was handed over to death, bore the sins of many, was vindicated by seeing the light of life, and resultantly makes many righteous."[33] Jesus was raised for the purpose of (*dia*) securing our justification. The death (cf. Rom. 3:24–25; 5:9) and resurrection of

32 In Acts 13:33 "by raising Jesus" God declares him to be his Son (quoting Ps. 2:7).

33 Michael F. Bird, *Romans*, SGBC 6 (Grand Rapids, MI: Zondervan Academic, 2016), 151–52. Further echoes of Isaiah can be heard in Rom. 5:19 (Isa. 53:11) and Rom. 15:21 (Isa. 52:15).

Jesus together accomplish what is needed for dealing with our sin and achieving our forgiveness and vindication. The resurrection is Jesus's own justification, God's declaration that he is innocent, and we are justified by our union with him in his death and resurrection.

Third, the resurrection of Jesus launches the new creation, as Jesus is "the firstborn among many brothers and sisters" (Rom. 8:29 NIV), or as Colossians 1:15 puts it, "firstborn over all creation" (CSB). Thomas Schreiner (commenting on 1:3–4) writes,

> The resurrection of Jesus Christ inaugurates the new age. When Jesus lived on earth as the Son of David, he lived his life in the old age of the flesh, which is characterized by weakness, sin, and death. At his resurrection, however, Jesus left the old age behind and inaugurated the new age of the Spirit.[34]

His resurrection displays the power and goodness of God. It is God's yes to the created order and sets in motion its renewal. Oliver O'Donovan explains, "In proclaiming the resurrection of Christ, the apostles proclaimed also the resurrection of mankind in Christ; and in proclaiming the resurrection of mankind, they proclaimed the renewal of all creation with him."[35]

Fourth, the resurrection of Jesus conquers evil. "In one sense this victory is achieved over God's personal adversary, the devil; in another the impersonal enemies of sin and death, resulting from human rebellion, are the defeated foes."[36] According to Romans, this victory is demonstrated in the resurrection of Christ from the dead, who was

- "appointed the powerful Son of God" (1:4 CSB);
- "raised for our justification" (4:25);
- "raised . . . at the right hand of God . . . interceding for us" (8:34).

34 Schreiner, *Romans,* 48.

35 Oliver O'Donovan, *Resurrection and Moral Order: An Outline for Evangelical Ethics* (Leicester, UK: Inter-Varsity Press, 1986), 31.

36 J. G. Millar, "Victory" in *NDBT* 831–32.

As Paul states, "We are more than conquerors through him who loved us" (8:37). This verse would be ringing in the ears of the Roman Christians when they heard Paul's bold assertion in 16:20 that the God of peace would soon complete his victory over Satan through them.

Finally, the resurrection of Jesus enables believers to "walk in newness of life" (6:4). (See chapter 11 on the believer's experience of the power of Christ's resurrection.)

The Ascension of Christ

Romans does not have a highly developed theology of the ascension of Jesus, a doctrine that is addressed more fully in Paul's other letters (e.g., 1 Cor. 15:24–28; Col. 3:1–4). However, the key ideas do appear, even if in passing. Paul connects Jesus's death, resurrection, exaltation, and intercession, listing them in chronological order: "Christ Jesus is the one who died—more than that, who was raised—who is at the right hand of God,[37] who indeed is interceding for us" (Rom. 8:34). Jesus's intercession for us is given some content in Hebrews: "He is able to save to the uttermost those who draw near to God through him, since he always lives to make intercession for them" (Heb. 7:25). "Christ's presence 'at the right hand of God' and his intercessory role guarantee that all God's elect will continue to find acceptance at the divine seat of judgment and be glorified in him."[38]

The Return of Christ

The teaching in Romans that Jesus will return to judge the world and bring salvation to those who trust in him is covered in chapter 14.

Conclusion

Paul proclaims at the beginning and end of Romans that his gospel is a message about Jesus Christ (1:3–4; 16:25). Romans explains who Jesus is and what he has done, is doing, and will do. He is the long-awaited

37 Cf. Ps. 110:1: "The Lord says to my Lord: / 'Sit at my right hand, / until I make your enemies your footstool.'"

38 Peterson, *Commentary on Romans,* 338.

Messiah, the Lord, the Son of God, the deliverer, the stone of stumbling, the last Adam, the servant to the circumcised, and God over all. Furthermore, his work is no less astounding and complete. Jesus died as our substitute, as our representative, to reveal the righteousness and love of God, and as an example of sacrificial love. Jesus rose from the dead to reveal his true identity, confirm our justification, inaugurate the new creation, conquer evil, and give us new life. Finally, Jesus ascended to make intercession for us while we await his final return in glory.

8

The Benefits of the Grace of God in the Gospel

We also rejoice in God.

ROMANS 5:11

IN THIS CHAPTER WE CONSIDER the benefits of being justified by faith—which, to risk an understatement, are considerable! Romans 5:1–11 is a key passage that we can use as a starting point for this topic. This text acts as a bridge and turning point between the first two major units of the letter. In Romans 1–4, Paul expounds the gospel of God's saving righteousness and the provision of a righteous status before God to those who believe in Jesus. Several verses in 5:1–11 summarize Romans 1–4 before moving the argument forward to the life of those who trust in Jesus:

- "We have been justified by faith" (5:1);
- "Christ died for the ungodly" (5:6);
- "Christ died for us. . . . We have now been justified . . . saved by him . . . [and] reconciled to God by the death of his Son" (5:8–10).

A Key Passage: Romans 5:1–11

The change in 5:1–11 is not only one of topic but also of tone. Paul moves from measured argument in Romans 1–4 where he uses mainly second-person verbs (e.g., 2:1: "You have no excuse") and third-person verbs (1:24: "God gave them up"; 4:2: "Abraham was justified") to exuberant enumeration of the blessings of the gospel using first-person plural verbs (5:1–2: "we have been justified"; "we rejoice in hope"). Three occurrences of the verb "to rejoice/boast" (5:2, 3, 11) mark the passage with a celebratory character. Paul moves from stern trial attorney to giddy schoolboy as he bounces from one idea to the next. He is excited about the benefits of being justified by grace through faith, and his enthusiasm is infectious.

In all, Paul boasts about seven such benefits: peace with God (5:1); access to God's grace (5:2); a sure hope (5:2–4); the joy of beneficial suffering (5:3–4); the gift of the Holy Spirit (5:5); the assurance of God's love (5:6–8); and, climactically, God himself (5:11).[1] The first six benefits overlap and turn out to be summed up in the seventh. They are introduced in this passage and developed in other parts of the letter. In particular, 8:18–39 forms an inclusio with 5:1–11.[2] They are best considered together, given that the subject of both passages is the hope of eternal life based on justification by faith despite present suffering (see table 8.1).

Table 8.1 Common Terms in Romans 5 and 8[a]

Common terms	Romans 5:1–11	Romans 8:18–39
"justify"	5:1, 9	8:30 (2x), 33
"save"	5:9–10	8:24
"love" (of God/Christ)	5:5, 8	8:35, 39

1 Four of the benefits are repeated in 15:13 in the form of a benediction: "May the God of *hope* fill you with all *joy* and *peace* in believing, so that by the power of *the Holy Spirit* you may abound in *hope*."

2 N. T. Wright, *Into the Heart of Romans: A Deep Dive into Paul's Greatest Letter* (London: SPCK, 2023), 179, says that when Paul returns to the theme of God's love at the end of Rom. 8, he "ties together the whole of chapters 5–8, looping back to 5.6–11 in a great arc."

Table 8.1 (*continued*)

Common terms	Romans 5:1–11	Romans 8:18–39
"glory"	5:2	8:18, 21, 30 ("glorify")
"hope"	5:2, 4, 5	8:20, 24 (4x), 25
"sufferings" (*thlipsis*)	5:3 (2x)	8:35 ("tribulation," *thlipsis*)
"endurance" (*hypomonē*)	5:3, 4	8:25 ("patience," *hypomonē*)

a The table is adapted (wording adjusted and rows reordered) from Douglas J. Moo, *The Letter to the Romans*, 2nd ed., NICNT (Grand Rapids, MI: Eerdmans, 2018), 318–19. Only "justify" (6:7) and "glory" (6:4) occur elsewhere in Rom. 5–8.

Two things about the seven benefits tie them inextricably to Paul's gospel. First, the centrality of Jesus Christ throughout both passages[3] reminds us that the gospel is about God's Son (1:3; 16:25). Second, the roots of the gospel in the Jewish Scriptures (1:2; 16:26) can be seen in that many of the benefits that bring such joy and confidence are the fulfillment of the hopes of Israel extended to the new people of God, including Gentiles.[4]

Benefits of Justification

Peace with God

The first benefit of being justified by faith and standing in God's grace is "peace with God" (Rom. 5:1).[5] A key term in Romans, the blessing of *peace* has a rich backstory, present and future dimensions, and ethical implications. In Romans 2:10 "peace" with God is an eschatological gift (along with "glory and honor"). But for those "who are self-seeking and do not obey the truth," the alternative is grim: "wrath and fury," "tribulation and distress" (Rom. 2:8–9). Indeed, in the Prophets, peace is

3 Cf., e.g., "through our Lord Jesus Christ" (5:1, 11) and "in Christ Jesus our Lord" (8:39).

4 Thomas R. Schreiner, *Romans*, 2nd ed., BECNT (Grand Rapids, MI: Baker Academic, 2018), 258: "All of these blessings, which belonged to Israel as God's people, are now the portion of those who are in Christ."

5 Cf. Acts 10:36: "the gospel of peace through Jesus Christ" (my translation).

a consistent feature of the end-time fulfilment of God's covenant promises. The coming "son," who is the "Prince of Peace," will rule "on the throne of David," and "of the increase of his government and of peace there will be no end" (Isa. 9:6–7). "The effect of righteousness will be peace" for God's people, who "will abide in a peaceful habitation"[6] (Isa. 32:17–18). More than just the absence of discord and hostility, peace with God connotes restored relationships with God and all people in a new creation. Peace appears elsewhere in Romans: God is "the God of peace" (Rom. 16:20), "to set the mind on the Spirit is life and peace" (8:6), and "the kingdom of God" is a matter of "righteousness and peace and joy in the Holy Spirit" (14:17). Believers, by implication, are to follow "the way of peace" (3:17), "live peaceably with all" (12:18), and "pursue what makes for peace" (14:19). Although the full experience of peace awaits the eschaton, Paul prays, "May the God of hope fill you with all joy and peace in believing" (15:13).

Access to God's Grace

The second benefit is "access by faith into this grace in which we stand" that comes through Jesus Christ (Rom. 5:2). Whereas Paul elsewhere uses the word "access" (*prosagōgē*) to describe entry into God's presence (Eph. 2:18; 3:12), in Romans 5:2 it refers to the continuing availability of God's "grace" (*charis*) to believers made possible by the work of Christ. In other words, "access" in 5:2 should not be limited to the gracious provision of the availability of God to hear our prayers. Rather, it refers to the security and ongoing blessing of those put right with God. We have continual access to the grace that saves us (Rom. 3:24); we are not only saved by grace but also strengthened and sustained by grace. "Access by faith into this grace" is the equivalent of the lifelong promise of 8:32: "He who did not spare his own Son but gave him up for us all, how will he not also with him graciously [*charisetai*] give us all things?" Such access to God and his grace is the fulfilment of Israel's temple and sacrificial system, a provision designed to give God's people

6 Cf. Isa. 48:20–22; 54:10–17; Ezek. 34:25; 37:26; Mic. 5:4–5; Hag. 2:9.

the blessings of his presence and mercy throughout their lives. At the beginning and end of Romans, Paul wishes that the Roman Christians experience God's grace in their lives together (1:7; 16:20).

A Sure Hope

The third benefit is the "hope of the glory of God" (5:2). "The major motif of the paragraph,"[7] the prospect of glory from God (a genitive of source) in the future is unsurprisingly something to celebrate, joyfully look forward to, and take pride in. The Greek verb in "we *rejoice* in hope of the glory of God" (5:2) is *kauchaomai*—"to boast" (see ESV margin note). This word can have both negative and positive connotations, and Paul exploits both poles of meaning in Romans. On the one hand, self-confident boasting as the basis for one's standing with God is prohibited (3:27; 4:2). But boasting in and joyfully praising God for his blessings—including hope—is entirely appropriate (5:2, 3, 11).

Paul understands that hope can seem a flimsy concept. Hope, by definition, is unrealized longing: "Now hope that is seen is not hope. For who hopes for what he sees?" (8:24).[8] Hopes differ in terms of the fervency of the desire in question and the realistic expectation of that desire being fulfilled. Some hopes are trivial; others unlikely to eventuate. You can hope for a pay raise, fine weather, or for a loved one's recovery from serious illness. Hoping for the glory of God is a profound longing to experience fully the nature and character of the true and living God, his goodness and grace. It is a yearning to be with God. A fitting cause for joyful celebration, this hope longs to see Adam's lost glory reinstated and our falling short of God's glory rectified (3:23).

The fulfilment of such hope might seem doubtful and unlikely. But the hope of the gospel combines deep desire and confident expectation. It is a sure and certain hope that will not lead to disappointment or "put us to shame [*kataischunō*]" (Rom. 5:5), for it is guaranteed by the love

7 Schreiner, *Romans*, 262.

8 "In hope [Abraham] believed against hope" (4:18).

of God (see further below). As Schreiner points out, such confidence is "rooted in the OT (Pss. 22:5; 25:3, 20; 119:116; Isa. 28:16), where those who trust in God are assured that they will be vindicated for placing their confidence in him."[9]

In Romans 8, Paul refers to the fulfilment of that hope—namely, believers being glorified with Christ (8:17–18, 21, 30). Such hope is shared by Gentiles who did not seek God (Rom. 15:12, quoting Isa. 11:10). Elsewhere in Romans, Christians are to "rejoice" (*chairō*) in this glorious "hope" (Rom. 12:12), waiting patiently for its fulfilment (8:25) along with all of creation (8:18–19). (We shall return to the theme of hope as an eschatological reality in chapter 14.)

Beneficial Suffering

If peace, access to God's grace, and a sure hope are self-evidently wonderful benefits, the fourth blessing of justification comes as something of a surprise: "Not only that, but we rejoice in our sufferings" (5:3). The word translated "sufferings," *thlipsis*, is a general term for all kinds of hardship and afflictions. Paul claims that we can be glad of our troubles not out of some perverse enjoyment of pain but because we know that they bring significant benefits: "Suffering produces endurance, and endurance produces character, and character produces hope" (5:3–4). Such reasoning, of course, assumes that we value highly living in a way that pleases God and that we long for the day of our redemption.

Romans 8:18–30 expands on this teaching: "For I consider that the sufferings [*ta pathēmata*] of this present time are not worth comparing with the glory that is to be revealed to us" (8:18). In 8:35–39 Paul lists some of the things that can afflict us—tribulation, distress, persecution, famine, nakedness, danger, sword, death—and, like 5:5, he lands on the assurance of "the love of God" for us "in Christ Jesus our Lord" (8:39) as the ground for being sure that we are "more than conquerors through him who loved us" (8:37).

9 Schreiner, *Romans*, 264.

Many readers of Romans, including commentators, understandably balk at the notion of rejoicing in hardship and feel the need to drain the idea of any emotional content. Believing that you can't command a feeling, they assume that joy must be an attitude and not a feeling.[10] This view assumes a noncognitive view of emotion, whereby feelings like joy are spontaneous, involuntary physiological changes in the body that the mind names. However, there is good evidence that Jews and Christians in the ancient world operated on the assumption of a cognitive view of emotion, believing that emotion is connected to cognition, which is also the predominant view in psychology today.[11] Put simply, a cognitive view of emotion says that you feel a certain way, at least in part, because you think in a certain way.

Hence in Romans 5 we rejoice because we know certain things. James uses the same reasoning: "Consider it a great joy, my brothers and sisters, whenever you experience various trials, because you know that the testing of your faith produces endurance" (James 1:2–3 CSB). Matthew Elliot notes that "Paul's view of joy is well summarized in Romans 5:1–11 . . . [where] we find a powerful mix of theology and emotion. The theological truths give Paul reason to rejoice at all times."[12] Of course, feeling joy by knowing certain things is not automatic; it requires thinking about them regularly, believing them wholeheartedly, and having them seep deeply into our lives and worldview.

The Gift of the Holy Spirit

The fifth benefit of being justified by faith appears in Romans 5:5: "God's love has been poured into our hearts *through the Holy Spirit* who has been given to us." There is a critical backstory to the gift of the Spirit

10 E.g., M. Bockmuehl, *The Epistle to the Philippians*, BNTC (Peabody, MA: Hendrickson, 1998), 59, commenting on Phil. 4:4: "Joy in the Lord is not a feeling but an attitude, and as such it can be positively commanded."

11 See Matthew Elliott, *Faithful Feelings: Emotion in the New Testament* (Leicester, UK: Inter-Varsity Press, 2005).

12 Elliot, *Faithful Feelings,* 175. Note that the command to rejoice in Phil. 4:4 is "in the Lord," a phrase laden with various gospel truths, such as "the Lord is at hand" (Phil. 4:5) and "the peace of God . . . will guard your hearts and minds in Christ Jesus" (4:7).

to all believers. In Joel the same verb "to pour out" (*ekcheō*) is used to describe the gift of the Spirit as the mark of the new age:

> And it shall come to pass afterward,
> that I will pour out my Spirit on all flesh;
> . . . .
> in those days I will pour out my Spirit. (Joel 2:28–29 [3:1–2 LXX]; cf. 1 Cor. 12:7; Acts 2:17, 18, 33; 10:45)

The Spirit of God gives believers the experience of the overflowing love of God, reassuring us of his care and concern in the midst of trials and providing a firm ground for hope. Paul returns to the work of the indwelling Spirit in Romans 8:1–11, a passage we will take up in chapter 9.

The Assurance of God's Love

The sixth benefit is being assured that God loves us, which is how Paul addressed the Christians in Rome "To all those in Rome who are loved by God" (Rom. 1:7). In 5:6–8 Paul provides "the objective grounds for the subjective experience of the love of God described in 5:5."[13] The death of Christ "for us" (5:8 [2x]; cf. 5:6) is the irrefutable proof that God loves us.[14] The completely undeserved and extraordinary nature of God's love is seen in three descriptions of those for whom Christ died: for "the ungodly" (5:6), "sinners" (5:8), and his "enemies" (5:10). It is also seen in contrast to two situations of human love where such sacrificial love is so unlikely and uncommon (5:7). Dying for us "at the right time" (5:6)[15] points to Christ's death as the climax of salvation history. Romans 8:31–39 makes a similar point about "the unshakeable and sovereign love of God."[16] The death of God's Son (8:32, 34) proves the love of Christ (8:35), the love of God (8:39), and the truth that God is "for us" (8:31).

13 David Abernathy, *An Exegetical Summary of Romans 1–8*, 2nd ed. (Dallas: SIL International, 2008), 364.

14 Cf. Gal. 2:20: "the Son of God, who loved me and gave himself for me."

15 Cf. Gal. 4:4: "when the fullness of time had come."

16 Michael F. Bird, *Romans*, SGBC 6 (Grand Rapids, MI: Zondervan Academic, 2016), 290.

God Himself

The unit culminates in 5:11 with the seventh benefit of being justified by faith: "More than that, we also rejoice in God through our Lord Jesus Christ, through whom we have now received reconciliation." Schreiner rightly draws a link with Romans 1: "The root sin is the refusal to honor and glorify God (1:21–23), whereas the result of righteousness is a heartfelt boasting in God that finds its greatest delight in him."[17]

Rejoicing in God himself is a fitting capstone to Paul's celebration of the benefits of salvation. Those who are justified, saved, and reconciled have peace with God, access to God's grace, the hope of the glory of God, an experience of suffering that leads them closer to God, the gift of God's Spirit, and the assurance of God's extraordinary love demonstrated in the death of God's Son. These six converge and reach their climax with Paul's final call to rejoice in God himself.

Conclusion

The benefits of the grace of God in the gospel are beyond measure. According to Romans 5:1–11 and 8:18–39, we rejoice in God the Father with whom we have peace, who loves us, and from whom we will receive glory. We rejoice in God the Son, who died for us, through whom we have peace with God, by whose blood we are justified, who saves us from God's wrath, and through whom we are reconciled. And we rejoice in God the Spirit, who continually assures us of God's unfailing and extraordinary love for us.

17 Schreiner, *Romans*, 259.

9

The Person and Work of the Holy Spirit

The Spirit is life.

ROMANS 8:10

THE WORK OF THE HOLY SPIRIT is a secondary doctrine in Romans. This is not because the Spirit is unimportant or plays a minor role but because the work of the Spirit intersects with many other doctrines and only comes close to a primary focus in 8:1–17. Accordingly, the Spirit's work is addressed in several chapters in this book. In this chapter, we survey the Spirit's role in the gospel in Romans by looking at (1) the person of the Spirit in connection with the Father and the Son and (2) the work of the Spirit in bringing various gospel blessings. As we will see, the person and work of the Spirit are of critical importance to several dimensions of Paul's gospel in Romans. If Jesus Christ is the central figure of the gospel, then the Holy Spirit is the essential means of receiving the blessings of the gospel.

The Person of the Spirit

Romans 1:2–4 not only contains seminal information about the gospel of God, its scriptural roots, and the Lord Jesus Christ but also introduces the person and work of the Spirit. All three members of the Trinity are mentioned in this gospel summary, and each is accorded a distinctive role or activity: (1) the source of the gospel is God, who is the Father (2) of the Lord Jesus Christ, who was born in the line of David and raised from the dead (3) by the Spirit of holiness. Thus, in the opening verses of the letter, we learn that the Spirit is associated with the Father and the Son, is characterized by and/or supplies holiness, and was the means of Jesus's resurrection.

In the second reference to the Spirit, Paul defines the true Jew as someone who pleases God by virtue of an inward work of the Spirit: "A Jew is one inwardly, and circumcision is a matter of the heart, *by the Spirit*, not by the letter" (Rom. 2:29). This text not only identifies a key work of the Spirit but also points to the fulfilment of Old Testament prophecies that predict a future messianic age when God's Spirit would be poured out "from on high" (Isa. 32:15) on Jacob's offspring (Isa. 44:3; cf. Joel 2:28–29), giving them "a new heart" and causing them to "walk in [his] statutes and . . . obey [his] rules" (Ezek. 36:26–27).

In Romans, "the Holy Spirit" (Rom. 5:5; 9:1; 14:17; 15:13, 16) is called both "the Spirit of God" (8:9, 14) and "the Spirit of Christ" (8:9). This close connection to the Father and the Son points to the Spirit's role of enabling us to encounter the triune God. Gordon Fee notes the coinherence of the three persons of the Godhead: "The Spirit is none other than the way the eternal God and his Christ have come to us in the present, as a personal presence taking up residence within the life of the believer."[1]

The cooperation and perfect alignment of the Spirit with the will of God and Christ is clearly seen when descriptions of their works overlap. For example, "the Spirit intercedes for the saints according to the will of God" (8:27), while Christ Jesus is "interceding for us" (8:34). The resurrection of the Son of God was by means of the Spirit (1:4; 8:11), and "Christ was raised from the dead by the glory of the

1 Gordon Fee, *God's Empowering Presence: The Holy Spirit in the Letters of Paul* (Grand Rapids, MI: Baker, 2009), 554.

Father" (6:4). In 8:1 believers are "in Christ Jesus," and in 8:9 they are "in the Spirit." Paul says that the Spirit pours "God's love" into our hearts (5:5), while he later appeals for prayer on his behalf "by the love of the Spirit" (15:30).

The close connection of the Spirit to God and God's Son, however, does not preclude the Spirit's distinct identity and activity. As we will see below, the Spirit's work in the life of believers covers everything from our initial salvation, to our progress in all aspects of the Christian life, to the hope of eternal life. Paul twice uses the intensive personal pronoun "himself" (*autos*) to underscore the Spirit's independent identity. In 8:26 the Spirit makes up for the shortcomings of our feeble and bewildered prayers:[2] "The Spirit *himself* intercedes for us with inexpressible groanings" (CSB). In 8:16 "the Spirit *himself* bears witness with our spirit that we are children of God." These two references, as L. Ann Jervis notes, "emphasize the activity of the Spirit and the Spirit alone."[3]

The Work of the Spirit

In Romans 1–4 the joint work of God and his Son in judgment and justification is the clear focus, with just two references to the Holy Spirit (1:4; 2:29; see above). However, in Romans 5–8 (especially Romans 8), the Spirit's involvement in the Christian life comes to the fore, followed by a few significant references in Romans 12–15. In Romans 5–15 the Spirit is associated with justification, adoption, prayer, the kingdom of God, righteousness, joy, peace, love, and hope. The two foundational ideas that stamp the work of the Spirit across the letter are holiness and new life.

Holiness

The frequent connection of the Spirit to holiness/sanctification (1:4; 15:16) is not just about his own purity. As Jervis observes, "The Spirit [in Romans] is holy and so transforms those whom it touches, by filling

2 "In our weakness . . . we do not know what to pray" (8:26).

3 L. Ann Jervis, "The Spirit Brings Christ's Life to Life," in *Reading Paul's Letter to the Romans*, ed. Jerry L. Sumney (Atlanta: SBL, 2012), 149.

hearts with God's love and love for God (5:5), by making Gentiles into godly/sanctified people, and by instilling hope."[4]

Paul contrasts two ways to live: "in the flesh," which indulges sin and leads to death, and "in the new way of the Spirit," which leads to serving God in freedom (7:5–6). With twelve references to the Spirit in 8:1–13, Paul then elaborates on life in the Spirit. Those who "walk . . . according to the Spirit" (8:4) and "set their minds on the things of the Spirit" (8:5) experience "life and peace" (8:6). In short, the Spirit sets believers free from sin and death (8:2) and enables them to live holy lives, pleasing to God (8:8).

Paul's apostolic commission involves "priestly service of the gospel of God," which he undertakes to bring an acceptable offering of the Gentiles, "sanctified by the Holy Spirit" (15:16). As Moo puts it,

> Paul regularly refers to the Spirit as the *Holy* Spirit. By doing so, he reminds us that we are people indwelt by one who is intrinsically holy, mediating to us the holiness of all the persons of the Godhead. At the same time, Paul implies the only possible source of Christian holiness comes through "the sanctifying work of the Spirit."[5]

Life

The connection between the Spirit and life is forged with reference to the resurrection of Jesus from the dead (1:4; 8:11). Paul makes the connection explicit when he says, "The Spirit is life" (8:10; cf. 8:2). "The Spirit is for and about life, even bringing life out of death."[6] The life that the Spirit gives has the shape of the life of Christ. For believers, this means being set free from the power of sin and death. Believers are like Christ in dying to sin and being made alive to God (6:10). "If you live according to the flesh you will die, but if by the Spirit you put to death the deeds of the body, you will live" (8:13). Because believers

4 Jervis, "The Spirit Brings Christ's Life to Life," 148.

5 Douglas J. Moo, *A Theology of Paul and His Letters: The Gift of the New Realm in Christ*, BTNT (Grand Rapids, MI: Zondervan Academic, 2021), 625.

6 Jervis, "The Spirit Brings Christ's Life to Life," 146.

are in union with Christ, the Spirit's life-giving work applies equally to Christ and Christians. Indeed, the Spirit makes us "sons of God" (8:14) and "fellow heirs with Christ" (8:17).

Justification

The Spirit's work for believers in Christ is not limited to the Christian life. "There is . . . no condemnation" of believers by God (i.e., they are justified) because they are "in Christ"—that is, in union with him—and set free "from the law of sin and death" by "the Spirit of life" (8:1–2). The Spirit's work extends from coversion to the end of life and beyond.

Adoption and Freedom

Adoption into God's family is perhaps the most comprehensive blessing of the gospel. Paul attributes our adoption to the work of the Spirit: "You have received the Spirit of adoption as sons. . . . The Spirit himself bears witness with our spirit that we are children of God" (8:15–16). This "solemn and emphatic statement about the Spirit's work"[7] appears in the context of being set free from "the spirit of slavery" (8:15). Such freedom means that we are no longer debtors to the flesh (8:12) and in slavery to sin and its dominion. Instead, the Spirit "confirms"[8] that believers are God's children (8:16), even "heirs of God and fellow heirs with Christ" (8:17), a status that leads believers to cry "Abba! Father!" (8:15). By supporting our prayers, the Spirit not only enables such intimate access to our heavenly Father but also engages our deepest emotions, thoughts, and desires (8:27: "searches our hearts"), ensuring the effectiveness of our prayers (8:27: "according to the will of God").

Righteousness, Peace, and Joy

In 14:17 Paul explains that the essential blessings of the present experience of the kingdom of God—"righteousness and peace and joy"—are

7 David G. Peterson, *Commentary on Romans*, BTCP (Nashville: Holman Reference, 2017), 318.

8 "Συμμαρτυρέω," in BDAG 957.

due to the Holy Spirit's agency (*en* plus the dative). In context, these three blessings describe the happy existence of the people of God that is put at risk by judging and despising other Christians about disputable matters (see chapter 11 below).

In Romans, peace is associated with God (15:33; 16:20), Jesus Christ (5:1), and the Spirit (14:17). According to Paul, peace from the Spirit "ends the internal 'warring' of the fleshly mind in Romans 7:23."[9] "For to set the mind on the flesh is death, but to set the mind on the Spirit is life and peace" (8:6). Craig Keener explains:

> For Paul, the "frame of mind involving the flesh" is the disposition or habitual way of thinking dominated by worldly, purely human concerns. Self-focused on one's personal bodily existence. . . . By contrast, the "frame of mind involving the Spirit" is a righteous mental lifestyle in which God's presence by the Spirit makes the decisive difference. This frame of mind involves life and peace, possibly evoking the context of Isaiah 26:3 ["You keep him in perfect peace / whose mind is stayed on you, / because he trusts in you"].[10]

The gospel brings peace with God, peace with others, and peace of mind.

Love

Paul instructs the Roman Christians to express genuine love (12:9) by, among other things, being "fervent in spirit" (12:11)—or "fervent in the Spirit" (CSB).[11] Though it is debated whether *pneuma* refers to the human spirit or the Spirit of God, the parallel with "serve the Lord" in 12:11 makes it likely that Paul meant the latter. In other words, he exhorts us "to be stirred up emotionally, be enthusiastic/excited/on fire"[12] by the Spirit. Such stirring prompts us to serve God and others in love.

9 Craig S. Keener, *The Mind of the Spirit: Paul's Approach to Transformed Thinking* (Grand Rapids, MI: Baker Academic, 2016), 135.

10 Keener, *The Mind of the Spirit*, 141.

11 Cf. ISV: "Be on fire with the Spirit."

12 "Ζέω," in BDAG 426.

We express love to others by being fervent in the Spirit in response to the experience of the Spirit's love for us (15:30) and God's love for us poured into our hearts by the Spirit (5:5).

Hope

The gift of the Spirit is a pledge of things to come: "And not only the creation, but we ourselves, who have the firstfruits of the Spirit, groan inwardly as we wait eagerly for adoption as sons, the redemption of our bodies. For in this hope we were saved" (8:23–24). "Redemption of our bodies" refers to "the final resurrection of our bodies at the parousia, our complete and final liberation."[13]

Graham Cole draws together critical aspects of the Spirit's work in Romans and lands on glory as the goal of the hope the Spirit provides (see 8:30):

> If the gift of the Spirit is the down payment (*arrabōn*) of the future and its beginnings (*aparchē*), what is the content of our hope? After all, according to Paul, it is the Spirit whose power enables believers to abound in hope (Rom. 15:13). The answer in Pauline terms is glory, as Romans 8 shows. "The Spirit of life" will give us life (Rom. 8:1–13). "The Spirit of adoption" will give us status (vv. 14–17). And the "Spirit of glory" will ultimately usher us into the final state of glorification. Then we shall be Spirit-shaped into the likeness of Christ.[14]

If Paul's purpose in Romans is to strengthen the Roman Christians by the gospel, it is no accident that he insists that his "ministry of the gospel" in bringing "the Gentiles to obedience" requires "the power of the Spirit of God" (15:18–19). To be strengthened by the gospel, believers need the power of the Spirit, who is the person of the Godhead who applies the work of Christ to our lives, brings us into God's family, and

13 C. E. B. Cranfield, *A Critical and Exegetical Commentary on the Epistle to the Romans: Introduction and Commentary on Romans 1–8*, ICC (Edinburgh: T&T Clark, 1975), 419.

14 Graham A. Cole, *He Who Gives Life: The Doctrine of the Holy Spirit*, FET (Wheaton, IL: Crossway, 2007), 239.

is the agent by whom God works to make us holy. It is by the power of the Holy Spirit that "the God of hope" fills us "with all joy and peace in believing" and enables us to "abound in hope" of eternal life (15:13).

Conclusion

Gordon Fee notes the distinctive roles of the three divine persons in planning, procuring, and implementing salvation: "God is the ground of all things and the one who raises the dead; Christ is the one who has brought righteousness; and the Spirit is the presence of both God and Christ in the present, thus giving life now and guaranteeing life for the future."[15] If the gospel is "the power of God for salvation" (1:16), it is no surprise that Paul points to the power of the Spirit (15:13, 19) in spreading the message and strengthening those who are saved.

15 Fee, *God's Empowering Presence*, 554.

10

Israel's Rejection of the Gospel

It is not as though the word of God has failed.

ROMANS 9:6

IN ROMANS 1–8 Paul demonstrates how Jesus Christ fulfills the promises of salvation that God had made to Israel. Then in Romans 9–11 he tackles the problem of Israel's failure to respond to the gospel. Far from an aside, Romans 9–11 addresses head-on some major concerns arising from his exposition of the gospel. If the gospel is "to the Jew first" (1:16), why has there been so little response among Jews? If the Jews enjoy so many privileges (3:1–2), what has happened to the divine promises to the patriarchs? Has God been unrighteous in this treatment of his chosen people? Paul offers an impassioned defense of the faithfulness of God and insists that "it is not as though the word of God has failed" (9:6). He argues that Israel's failure is due to her own unbelief (9:1–10:21), is not universal in scope (11:1–10), and is not permanent or final (11:11–32). Despite Israel's rejection of the righteousness of God by faith and God's temporary national rejection of them, God remains faithful to his covenant promises to Israel.

No passage in the New Testament does more to explain and extol the sovereignty, justice, grace, and mercy of God than Romans 9–11. It also presents some challenging questions of interpretation. In addition to the exegetical problems, the key question to keep in focus is what the passage teaches about the character of God. We will consider its profound theology by looking at the three central subjects: (1) the inclusion of the Gentiles, (2) divine election to salvation, and (3) gospel hope for Israel. All three are critical aspects of Paul's gospel that he tackles with copious references to the Old Testament.[1] In the following discussion, Romans 9–11 will be read in conjunction with other parts of the letter.

The Inclusion of the Gentiles

In defending the righteous character of God in Romans 9–11, Paul has to deal not just with the unexpectedly disappointing response of Jews to the gospel (9:1–3; 10:1) but also with the relative success of the Gentile mission that led to churches being dominated by Gentiles—including the Roman church (1:6, 15). The full inclusion of Gentile believers into the people of God is one of the central themes of Romans, appearing across the letter, not just in Romans 9–11. As Schreiner demonstrates, the theme of the inclusion of Gentiles in God's saving promises is introduced in the opening chapters: The gospel is for the Jew first but also for the Greek (1:16; 2:10). Gentiles who observe the law are on the same level as circumcised Jews who keep it (2:25–29). Both Jews and Gentiles are under the condemnation of sin (3:9–20, 23). God's saving righteousness is available "for all who believe. For there is no distinction" (3:22). God justifies both Jews and Gentiles in the same way (3:28–30). Abraham is the father of both Jews and believing Gentiles (4:9–12). Paul divides humanity in terms of being in Adam or in Christ (5:12–21); thus, all those in Christ, whether Jew or Gentile, belong to the people of God.[2] "Throughout Romans Paul is keen to show how the good news extends to gentiles."[3]

1 One third of the quotations of Scripture in Paul's letters appear in Rom. 9–11, and one third of Rom. 9–11 is comprised of those quotations.

2 Thomas R. Schreiner, *Paul, Apostle of God's Glory in Christ: A Pauline Theology*, 2nd ed. (Downers Grove, IL: IVP Academic, 2020), 255.

3 Douglas J. Moo, *A Theology of Paul and His Letters: The Gift of the New Realm in Christ*, BTNT (Grand Rapids, MI: Zondervan Academic, 2021), 233.

Romans 9–11 gives the fullest explanation of the inclusion of Gentiles in the people of God in the letter. Paul insists that, just as God is free to save only some Israelites (Rom. 9:6–13, 27–29), he is also free to save many Gentiles: "Those who were not my people I will call my people" (Rom. 9:25, quoting Hos. 2:23; cf. Rom. 9:26, quoting Hos. 1:10). Paul writes, "Gentiles who did not pursue righteousness have attained it, that is, a righteousness that is by faith" (Rom. 9:30), and he quotes God as saying,

> I have been found by those who did not seek me;
>   I have shown myself to those who did not ask for me.
>   (Rom. 10:20, quoting Isa. 65:1)

According to Paul, "there is no distinction between Jew and Greek; for the same Lord is Lord of all, bestowing his riches on all who call on him. For 'everyone who calls on the name of the Lord will be saved' " (Rom. 10:12–13, quoting Joel 2:32). Paul links salvation for the Gentiles to the failure of Israel to believe the gospel: "Through their trespass salvation has come to the Gentiles" (Rom. 11:11; cf. 11:15, 25–26, 30–31). Using the image of an olive tree with the patriarchs as the root, Paul explains that natural branches (Israel) have been broken off and wild shoots (Gentiles) have been grafted into the vine (Rom. 11:17–24).

When Paul writes of the grace that God had given to him, he points to his commission to be a preacher of the gospel to Gentiles: "through whom *we have received grace* and apostleship to bring about the obedience of faith for the sake of his name among all the nations" (1:5); "*the grace given me by God* to be a minister of Christ Jesus to the Gentiles" (15:15–16). Elsewhere in Romans, Paul identifies believers in Christ, both Jews and Gentiles, as the new people of God using designations and concepts that one would expect a Jew to apply strictly to fellow Jews: "God's elect" (8:33), "called" (1:6–7; 8:28, 30; 9:24), "saints" (1:7), "loved/beloved" (1:7; 9:25), children of Abraham (4:11–12, 16–17), and the true circumcision (2:28–30). The epitome of the grace of God for Paul is the admission of Gentiles, people without God and without hope, to the glorious privileges that had been exclusive to Israel. The full inclusion of the Gentiles to the people of God was for Paul—and remains to this day—the greatest expression of the amazing grace of God. Believers from a Gentile background should never forget that they were grafted into God's historic, chosen people and, as a result, should be humble (11:13–14, 20–21, 25) and thankful forever.

Divine Election to Salvation

A significant part of Paul's explanation for both Gentile inclusion and Jewish failure to respond is divine election. Romans 9–11 is the longest passage in the Bible on the knotty but important question of God's sovereignty and human responsibility. It is a complicated unit and appears in numerous theological debates. In my understanding, these chapters teach five things about divine election. As we will see below, God's election (1) is by grace alone, (2) is of individuals to salvation, (3) is certain, (4) is compatible with human choice and responsibility, and (5) engenders a big view of God.

Indeed, much of this can be seen (before Rom. 9–11) in Paul's precis of the process of salvation in 8:29–30: "Those whom he [God] foreknew he also predestined to be conformed to the image of his Son, in order that he might be the firstborn among many brothers. And those whom he predestined he also called, and those whom he called he also justified, and those whom he justified he also glorified." These two verses narrate in chronological order five salvific actions of God: He foreknows, predestines, calls, justifies, and glorifies certain people. That the same group is in view at each stage is made clear by the repetition of "those whom" and "also." There is no leakage from start to finish; all of those foreknown will be glorified. *Foreknowing* does not concern knowing about someone or what they might do but, rather, knowing them personally in advance (cf. 11:2)[4]—that is, God setting his love on them. *Predestination* refers to God's purpose to make them like

4 E.g., "Before I formed you in the womb I knew you" (Jer. 1:5). "You only have I known of all the families of the earth" (Amos 3:2).

Christ. *Calling*, as we will see in Romans 9–11 below, is a synonym for God's choice of them. *Justification* is about their being put right with God (a status received by faith: 3:25, 28; 4:5; 5:1). God has purposed to bring to a glorious destiny those who love God in response to his call (8:28). In context, the passage is an encouragement to endure suffering in the present (8:18–27). For Paul God's election is not a subject for philosophical speculation but an encouraging doctrine of pastoral comfort and significance.

Divine election is a matter of *God's grace alone*. In 9:7–13 Paul refers to God choosing Isaac over Ishmael and choosing Jacob over Esau to make clear that God's election rests on "him who calls" (9:11). In both cases election is unrelated to deeds: "Though they were not yet born and had done nothing either good or bad—in order that God's purpose of election might continue, not because of works but because of him who calls" (9:11). The decisive nature of God's grace is also apparent in 9:14–18, where Paul insists that it is God's prerogative to have mercy and compassion on whomever he wills and that election does not depend on human will or exertion. Romans 11:5–6 explicitly links election to grace: There is "a remnant, chosen by grace . . . [and] if it is by grace, it is no longer on the basis of works; otherwise grace would no longer be grace."[5] In fact, *mercy* is the key term throughout. Paul uses the noun "mercy" (*eleos*) and the verbs for "to show mercy" (*eleeō* and *eleaō*) a combined nine times in Romans 9–11 (9:15 [2x], 16, 18, 23; 11:30, 31 [2x], 32) and only twice elsewhere in the letter (12:8; 15:9). In Paul's mind, divine election underscores God's sovereignty, as well as his grace, mercy, and love.

Divine election in Romans 9–11 refers not only to nations (e.g., Israel [Jacob] in 9:13) or the roles people play in salvation history (e.g., Pharaoh in 9:17) but also to the *salvation of individuals*. Moo notes three points in the unit that "argue for some application [of election in Rom. 9–11] to the salvation of individuals."[6] First, Paul uses many

5 In 9:13 and 9:25 God's election is motivated by his love.

6 Moo, *A Theology of Paul and His Letters*, 231.

terms in Romans 9 that are used in discussions of salvation elsewhere in the letter, such as "children of God" and "children of the promise" (9:8), "calls" (9:11), "not because of works" (9:11), "wrath" (9:22), and "mercy" and "glory" (9:23). Second, Paul is addressing the following question throughout the unit: Who is included in God's people? This is the issue raised in 9:1–3 and 10:1, where Paul laments the failure of most of his fellow Jews to believe in Christ Jesus. Third, it is God's sovereign election to salvation that evokes the following questions: "Is there injustice on God's part?" (9:14) and "Why does [God] still find fault?" (9:19).

Divine election is according to God's sovereign will and, therefore, *certain*. The answer to the rhetorical question in 9:19—"Who can resist [God's] will?"—is an emphatic "No one." Here, God's "will" refers to "the purposeful intention of God"[7] and must be distinguished from his revealed or moral will (2:18; 12:2),[8] which refers to his desires for humanity that will not necessarily come to pass due to evil. Correspondingly, Paul uses the language of "calling" to underscore the certainty of those whom God chooses and who respond in faith. The gospel calling in such contexts is one that accomplishes what it invites. (We saw this in the discussion of 8:29–30 above.) Election depends on "him who calls" (9:11). Indeed, Paul can use "the called" as synonymous with "the chosen," as in 1 Corinthians 1:26–27: "Consider your calling. . . . God chose [you]."

Divine election is *compatible with human choice and responsibility*. Romans 9–11 makes abundantly clear that "when believers seek to clarify the reason for their salvation . . . they attribute it to God's electing work."[9] This realization renders the notion that they somehow deserve God's grace as inconceivable, and it ought to lead to genuine humility (11:18) and praise for God's mercy (11:33–36). Paul does not consider this emphasis on the sovereignty of God, however, to absolve human

7 "Βούλημα," in *TDNT* 1:637.

8 Cf. 1 Thess. 4:3: "This is the will of God, your sanctification: that you abstain from sexual immorality."

9 Schreiner, *Paul, Apostle of God's Glory in Christ*, 260.

beings of responsibility for their behavior, nor does it make responding to the gospel some charade. Although salvation depends on God, who "has mercy on whomever he wills, and . . . hardens whomever he wills" (9:18), the gospel is still about "a righteousness that is by faith" (9:30), a message that calls for one to confess the lordship of Christ and believe that God raised him from the dead (10:9–10). And this gospel entails a universal offer of salvation: "Everyone who calls on the name of the Lord will be saved" (Rom. 10:13, quoting Joel 2:32). Paul sees no contradiction between the sovereignty of God and human responsibility nor any reason to water down either.[10]

Paul's main concern in wrestling with the problem of Jewish unbelief in the gospel and the inclusion of the Gentiles in Romans 9–11 is to defend the character of God. What emerges is a vision of the glory, power, and wisdom of God—in short, *a big view of God*. When confronted with questions about how divine election impacts the justice of God, Paul underscores the fact that God is God and can do what he likes: "Who are you, O man, to answer back to God?" (9:20). Throughout Romans 9–11, Paul refers to the character of God to explain Israel's unbelief, election according to grace, and future hope (see below). Such references include the mercy (9:15, 16, 18, 23; 11:30, 31, 32), compassion (9:15), wrath (9:22), power (9:22; 11:23), glory (9:23; 11:36), love (9:25; 11:28), righteousness (10:3), grace (11:5, 6), kindness (11:22), severity (11:22), wisdom (11:33), and knowledge (11:33) of God.

The purpose of Romans 9–11 is not simply to explain the place of Israel and Gentiles in God's gospel plan but to lead us to humble praise and adoration of God. Reading Romans 9–11 raises some deep questions, some of which Paul poses himself (e.g., 9:14, 19; 10:14; 11:1, 7, 11). Despite such challenges, to read Romans 9–11 and not respond with awe of the sovereign God is to misread the passage. This is clear

10 Paul's posture is paralleled elsewhere in the New Testament. Acts 2:22–23, for example, shows double agency at work: divine sovereignty and human action regarding Christ's crucifixion. Significantly, the crowds who heard did not think that divine sovereignty absolved them of responsibility: "Now when they heard this they were cut to the heart" (Acts 2:37).

from the closing doxology in 11:33–36. John Piper points out the role these verses serve in the broader argument of Romans: "This is where God wants us to be when we have heard Romans 1–11. Amazed at mercy, and worshipping God through Jesus Christ. This is the response that will make us able to live out the practical moral demands of Romans 12–15."[11]

Praise and Worship in Romans

Romans 9–11 is widely regarded as a theological masterpiece. In just three chapters, Paul plumbs the depths of the wisdom and knowledge of God, addressing not only the place of Israel in God's purposes but also the doctrines of election and reprobation and of divine sovereignty and human responsibility. Yet the closing verses of this section are a doxology of praise to God that declares God's ways to be "unsearchable" and "inscrutable" (11:33). The longest doxology in his letters, it begins with a surprised interjection, includes three rapturous exclamations and three humbling rhetorical questions, and closes with a solemn amen to invite the readers' assent:

> Oh, the depth of the riches and wisdom and knowledge of God! How unsearchable are his judgments and how inscrutable his ways!
>
> "For who has known the mind of the Lord,
> or who has been his counselor?"
> "Or who has given a gift to him
> that he might be repaid?"

11 John Piper, "From God, to God, through God" (sermon, Bethlehem Baptist Church, Minneapolis, MN, March 28, 2004), https://www.desiringgod.org/.

For from him and through him and to him are all things.
To him be glory forever. Amen. (Rom. 11:33–36)

Having composed a profound reflection on the most enigmatic actions of God, Paul confesses that his thoughts fall short of fully grasping the mind of God. Paul doesn't doubt the truth of what he teaches but, rather, admits that in the end the knowledge of God is beyond human comprehension. The conclusion to Romans 9–11 demonstrates that the ultimate goal of understanding and believing the gospel is not to figure out God but to arrive at awestruck incredulity and joyful confidence in God. It is to be blown away in wide-eyed, transfixed adoration. The aim is not to achieve accurate eloquence but to become lost for words in the praise and wonder of God.

More than Paul's other letters, Romans is punctuated by praise and wonder. Rather than serving as perfunctory, pious gestures to break up the text, such notes of worship are central to the message and argument of Romans. Let us consider Paul's five doxologies, five notes of thanksgiving, and stirring call to worship.

Doxologies. Five of the fifteen occurrences of the word *amen* in Paul's letters appear in Romans as the conclusions to doxologies. The frequency of these ascriptions of glory to God is explained by the first and shortest in 1:25, which sets the scene for the other four. Paul concludes his condemnation of the sin of idolatry with an easily overlooked relative clause: "Claiming to be wise, . . . they exchanged the truth about God for a lie and worshiped and served the creature rather than the Creator, *who is blessed forever! Amen*" (1:22, 25). With these words, Paul not only distances himself from false worship but also models for his readers how turning from idols to the living and true God should lead to true worship (cf. 1 Thess. 1:9). The subsequent four doxologies in Romans recall the first and give glory to

God as sovereign (9:5); as Creator, sustainer, and goal of the universe (11:36); as the one who provides peace (15:33); and as the only wise God (16:27; cf. 1:23).

Thanksgiving. Paul highlights giving thanks five times in the letter. Gentiles are guilty not only of idolatry and sexual immorality but also ingratitude: "For although they knew God, they did not honor him as God *or give thanks to him*" (1:21). Paul shows a better way of responding to God when he gives thanks for the Roman Christians (1:8), for their heartfelt obedience to the gospel (6:17), and for what God has accomplished in Christ (7:25). He also commends Christians eating or abstaining from food with thanksgiving to God (14:6).

Call to worship. The idea of Paul as leader of worship in Romans hits its crescendo in 15:8–11, where he quotes three Old Testament passages that call on Gentiles to praise, extol, rejoice, and sing to the Lord with all God's people. In Romans, worship is an essential response to the gospel.[a]

a The theme of worship in Romans is developed further in 12:1–2 where Paul calls for "spiritual worship" (12:1) in our daily conduct before God.

Gospel Hope for Israel

After Paul argues that Israel's failure is due to unbelief (9:1–10:21), he then asks the obvious question: "Has God rejected his [chosen] people?" (11:1). His answer is an emphatic no: "God has not rejected his people whom he foreknew" (11:2), those on whom he set his love. Israel is "beloved [of God] for the sake of their forefathers" (11:28), the patriarchs to whom God gave promises and entered into binding covenants. That there is hope for Israel is based on the fact that "the word of God has not failed" (9:6)[12] and that "the gifts [of adoption, the

12 "The word of God" for Paul usually denotes the gospel message (cf. 1 Cor. 2:1; 14:36; 2 Cor. 2:17; 4:2; Col. 1:25; 1 Thess. 2:13; 2 Tim. 2:9). However, in this context, immediately

covenants, and the promises to Israel (3:1–2; 9:4–5)] and calling of God [of Israel to be his people] are irrevocable" (11:29). Hope for Israel can be seen in that Israel's failure is not universal in scope (11:1–10) and Israel's failure is not permanent or final (11:11–32).

In 11:1–10 Paul cites the election of a remnant within Israel as proof that God has not rejected his historic people. "The elect obtained" (11:7) what the majority of Israel failed to obtain—namely, a right standing with God. Paul cites his own experience as exhibit A. Lionel Windsor writes that in 11:1 ("I myself am an Israelite"), "Paul describes himself in terms of Israel's vocation. . . . This description of Paul as a paradigmatic Israelite provides the hinge for Israel's transition from a negative role to a positive role in God's worldwide purposes."[13] Romans 11:11 makes this point: "Through their trespass salvation has come to the Gentiles."

Furthermore, in 11:11–32 Paul stresses not only that Israel's failure led to the inclusion of many Gentiles into God's people but also that "the infusion of gentiles is designed by God ultimately to affect Jews—stimulating them to 'envy' or 'jealousy' and bringing many of them to salvation."[14] As Paul writes, "By the mercy shown to you [Gentiles] they [the Jews] also may now receive mercy" (11:31). This "plot twist"[15] is explained in 11:25–31, where Paul intimates that at some point in some way "all Israel will be saved" (11:26). Unfortunately, this is one of the most debated texts in Romans—in terms of not only what Paul means by "all Israel" but also when and how they get saved.

Let us take the issues one by one. Paul consistently uses "Israel" in his letters to refer to Israel in a national or ethnic sense.[16] The reference to

---

following the rehearsal of Israel's privileges in Rom. 9:4–5, it refers to the promises made to Israel.

13 Lionel J. Windsor, *Paul and the Vocation of Israel: How Paul's Jewish Identity Informs His Apostolic Ministry, with Special Reference to Romans*, BZNW 205 (Berlin: de Gruyter, 2014), 247.

14 Moo, *A Theology of Paul and His Letters*, 235.

15 Michael F. Bird, *Romans*, SGBC 6 (Grand Rapids, MI: Zondervan Academic, 2016), 390. Paul calls it "this mystery" (11:25).

16 Paul's statement that "not all who are descended from Israel belong to Israel" (9:6), rather than serving as a reference to all believers in Christ, is a reference to a believing remnant within Israel, given the prior context of 9:1–5.

"Israel" in the previous verse (11:25), supports this conclusion. However, "all Israel" is unlikely to mean every Israelite, given that the phrase is "used in the Old Testament often as a representative summary of the people (see, e.g., Josh 7:25; 2 Sam 16:22)."[17] As to the manner ("in this way," *houtos*) in which they will be saved, this occurs when "the Deliverer will come from Zion" (11:26)—that is, at the return of Jesus. Putting the pieces together, "we can say that 'all Israel' refers to ethnic Israel, a future salvation is promised for them, and this salvation is a future event that will become a reality when Jesus returns or near his return."[18]

Conclusion

While Romans 1–8 leads us to a deep assurance that God loves us intimately and personally as his adopted children, Romans 9–11 reminds us that God is not to be taken lightly. In response to Israel's disappointing failure to respond to the gospel, Paul offers a robust defense of the unchanging character of the sovereign, faithful, wise, and merciful God.

17 Moo, *A Theology of Paul and His Letters*, 236.

18 Thomas R. Schreiner, *Romans*, 2nd ed., BECNT (Grand Rapids, MI: Baker Academic, 2018), 605.

11

The Gospel and the Christian Life

Let not sin therefore reign in your mortal body.

ROMANS 6:12

THE GOSPEL OF GOD that Paul expounds in Romans is not solely about escaping the wrath of God at the final judgment. Whereas much of the salvation language in Romans refers to future deliverance (e.g., 5:9, 10; 10:9; 11:26; 13:11), several salvation ideas have present implications for the daily lives of believers: Being declared righteous before God provides a basis for obedience to God, "which leads to righteousness" in daily living (6:16). Redemption includes being emancipated from the power of sin (3:24). Freedom includes being liberated from the dominion of sin (6:18, 22; 8:2). Being adopted into God's family is the basis for putting sin to death (8:13–15). And union with Christ is the foundation for ending the reign of sin in our mortal bodies (see further below). Indeed, salvation in Romans means that believers in Christ are saved from both the penalty and the power of sin.

In chapters 11–13, we explore Paul's vision of the Christian life as an essential part of his gospel. Chapter 12 covers relating to one another in the body of Christ, and chapter 13 looks at behavior toward outsiders. In this chapter, we examine three foundational truths that underpin Christian living in Romans: union with Christ, life in the Spirit, and the imitation of Christ. These are three ways in which the gospel enables believers to end the reign of sin over their lives.

Dying and Rising in Union with Christ

In chapter 7 we noted the critical gospel truth of union with Christ and the related idea of Christ dying and rising as our representative. Here I wish to point out the relevance of dying with Christ (to the power of sin) and rising with Christ (to new life in him) to the task of not letting sin reign in our mortal bodies (6:12). The key passage is 6:1–23.

Romans 6 is a declaration of what believers have become in Christ and, consequently, why believers must not go on living in sin. The passage has a clear structure reflecting the indicative/imperative logic of Paul's ethics. Romans 6:1–11 and 6:15–23 are parallel units, both opening with a false inference that the grace of God leads to further sin, followed by appeals to the baptism of believers and our slavery to righteousness, respectively. Paul supplies the imperative to act in accordance with these truths: "Present yourselves to God as those who have been brought from death to life" (6:13). Believers are to live in ways that express their new identity in Christ.

Paul's appeal to baptism (6:3) is about its ongoing significance. Baptism here "recalls the entire event of conversion and initiation . . . [and] is the sign and seal that believers have entered into the story of Jesus' death and resurrection, and its liberating power is manifested in them."[1] Baptism marks us out as those joined to Christ. Along with initiation into the Christian life, baptism speaks of our ongoing life in Christ. Having risen with Christ, we "walk in newness of life" now (6:4). Being baptized (and recalling our baptism when others are baptized), reminds us of our need to put on Christ and to imitate him in everyday life.

The fact that we have been set free from sin's power by dying and rising with Christ negates despair and insecurity in our experience. On the other hand, that we are to resist sin's ongoing hold on our lives negates pride and overconfidence. The indicatives show that the impera-

1 Michael F. Bird, *Romans*, SGBC 6 (Grand Rapids, MI: Zondervan Academic, 2016), 196.

tives of Christlike living are not optional; the imperatives show that the indicatives do not make progress in ending sin's reign automatic. The logic of Paul's ethics may be summed up as this: Know who you are in Christ and the story to which you belong; behave accordingly.

Life in the Spirit

In Romans 8 Paul expounds the Spirit-directed life. But the full picture of life in the Spirit requires that Paul first deal with the alternative—namely, living under the law: He tells the Roman Christians that they are "not under law but under grace" (6:14), and he asserts (controversially for a Jew) that "the law came in to increase the trespass" (in 5:20). Then, Paul explains in Romans 7 that the law does not produce a life of fruitful obedience, but he also clarifies that he is not thereby denigrating God's law.

Paul uses the analogy of marriage to support his insistence that believers are not under the law (7:1–6). After noting a legal principle that "the law is binding on a person only as long as he lives" (7:1), he illustrates this principle in connection with marriage law: A married woman is only bound by law to her husband while he lives; if he dies, she is free to marry another man (7:2–3). Paul applies this lesson to believers in Christ: They had a binding relationship to the law but, having "died to the law through the body of Christ," they are free to be united to the living Lord (7:4). Then, he offers a preview and summary of 7:7–8:30 (7:5–6).

The interpretation of Romans 7:7–25 is a subject of considerable debate. Put simply, when Paul writes, "I am of the flesh, sold under sin" (7:14), and speaks in the first person throughout the passage, is he speaking as a non-Christian or as a Christian? Some argue that being "sold under sin" (7:14) and the lack of references to the Spirit until Romans 8 point to Paul recalling his life of unbelief under the law. In this case Romans 7 is the problem to which Romans 8 is the gospel solution.[2] Others see all of Romans 5–8 addressing the Christian life.

2 This view does not necessarily deny that there is a struggle with sin in the Christian life, pointing to parts of Rom. 8 and the ongoing conflict of the flesh and the Spirit (cf. Gal. 5).

In this view the depiction of the Christian's ongoing struggle with sin is supplemented with the depiction of life in the Spirit in Romans 8.

Romans 7 is both an apology for the law and also a dramatic presentation of the Christian's radical moral disability without the work of the Spirit.[3] In 7:7–13 Paul asserts that the law exposes and incites our sin, promising life but leading to death. However, the law is not sinful but rather holy, righteous, and good. In defending the law, Paul points to himself as the real culprit. Will Timmins offers this interpretive translation: "We (you Christians in Rome, and I the apostle Paul) know that the law is spiritual, but I (Paul) am fleshly, having been sold under sin." Timmins rightly observes, "Clearly the 'I' of the second part of the sentence is part of the 'we' of the first part."[4]

"Sold under sin" in 7:14 describes Paul's condition in his mortal body of being "fleshly." Timmins explains,

> Paul isn't saying he's a slave of sin and contradicting what he just said about the believer's freedom in chapter 6. We now have freedom through union with Christ in his death and resurrection (6:1–10), but our *bodies* don't yet share Christ's risen life (6:11). So there's still a slavery in our bodily members (7:23) as we await the redemption of our bodies (8:23). That's what it means to be fleshly.[5]

While we remain in the body, we await the full manifestation of who we are in Christ. Sin impairs our ability to accomplish what is good (7:15, 18, 19), and we cannot obey the law (7:16, 18, 19, 21). Sin living within believers (7:17, 20) affects all of our bodily members (7:23). This is the universal human condition, and one that Christians perceive and experience. Such a bleak but realistic diagnosis protects Christians from self-deception and a naïve triumphalism. It reminds us of our

3 See Will N. Timmins, *Romans 7 and Christian Identity: A Study of the 'I' in Its Literary Context*, SNTSMS (Cambridge: Cambridge University Press, 2017).

4 Will Timmins, "What's Really Going On in Romans 7?," The Gospel Coalition, July 2, 2018, https://www.thegospelcoalition.org/.

5 Timmins, "What's Really Going On in Romans 7?," (emphasis in original).

profound need for God and to be set free by him from the law of sin (7:25; 8:2). It is the necessary first step to "put to death the deeds of the body" (8:13). Romans 7 and 8 strike the healthy balance between the already and not yet of Christian existence.

In Romans 8, Paul expounds the work of the Spirit in our lives. The Spirit gives believers assurance that they are children of God now (8:14–17) and have a sure hope of glory in the future (8:18–30), twin assurances that merit exuberant celebration (8:31–39). In the present, life in the Spirit is the way believers can overcome sin in their lives (8:1–13).

The Spirit sets believers "free in Christ Jesus from the law of sin and death" (8:2), delivering them from the rule that sin must lead to death, a deliverance made possible by Jesus's dying for us "as a sin offering" (8:3 ESV margin note).[6] The Spirit enables believers to "walk [in daily conduct] not according to the flesh but according to the Spirit" (8:4). The Spirit dwelling in us gives life to our mortal bodies (8:11), as we orient our thinking to the Spirit rather than the flesh (8:4–7) and "put to death the deeds of the body" (8:13).

Conformed to the Image of God's Son

If the gospel is about Jesus Christ (1:3; 16:25), how central is the imitation of Christ in the life of believers? While there is no explicit call to follow the example of Christ (such as in 1 Cor. 11:1; Phil. 2:5; 1 Thess. 1:6), the imitation of Christ actually plays a major role in Paul's vision of the Christian life in Romans. We will consider the key text (Rom. 8:29), seven additional texts that fill out the picture, and two key terms for the Christian life that are associated with the example of Christ.

Romans 8:29 is the key text for imitating Christ. In the midst of a comforting passage (8:28–30), Paul explains the purpose of predestination: "to be conformed to the image of [God's] Son, in order that he might be the firstborn among many brothers [and sisters]" (8:29). Though debated, it is better to take this text as referring to our present

6 Greek *peri hamartias*, which regularly denotes the sin offering in LXX Lev. 4:3, 14; 6:23; 7:7, 37; 8:2, 14; 9:2–3, 7, 10, 15, 22; 10:16–17, 19; 12:6, 8; 14:13, 19, 22, 31; 15:15, 30; 16:3, 5–6, 9, 11, 15, 25, 27; 19:22; 23:19.

moral renovation rather than only our future eschatological transformation. The language of being "transformed" (*metamorphorphoō*) in our behavior in 12:2 echoes the goal of being "conformed" (*summorphos*) to the image of God's Son in 8:29.[7] The context of Romans 8:29 also favours seeing the present transformation of believers. The theme of the weakness and suffering of believers pervades all of Romans 8 and is brought to a sharp point in 8:28 with the reference to "all things work[ing] together for good" for God's people. The most likely referent of "all things" is our weakness and groaning in the previous verses and the trouble and hardship in the ensuing context.

The theme of being conformed to the image of God's Son is then echoed elsewhere in Romans. We are to imitate Christ by suffering as he suffered (8:17). Behavioral transformation requires becoming a living sacrifice (12:1–2), recalling the cultic language describing Jesus's atoning death (3:24–25; 5:8–9; 8:3–4). The charge to "put on the Lord Jesus Christ" (13:14) is a call to Christlike behavior: "cast off the works of darkness" (13:12) and "walk properly as in the daytime" (13:13). "Walking in love" is linked to the example of Christ's love in dying for us (14:15). Believers are told to forsake selfish behavior by following the example of Christ, who "did not please himself" (15:3)—a colossal understatement given Christ's death on a cross for us! Paul bases his call to unity among Christians on having "the same attitude of mind toward each other that Christ Jesus had" (15:5 NIV). Believers are to "welcome one another as Christ has welcomed you" (15:7). Even if some of these connections are less certain than others, their cumulative weight demonstrates that Paul's teaching is both aligned with and inspired by the conduct of Jesus Christ.

Two key terms that Paul uses in Romans for characterizing the Christian life reinforce the theme of imitating Christ. First, *obedience* is not only the appropriate response to the gospel (cf. 15:18) but also

7 The verb *metamorphorphoō* also appears in 2 Cor. 3:18, where believers are being "transformed" into Christ's image with ever increasing glory. And *summorphizō* (the verb cognate of the noun in Rom. 8:29) appears in Phil. 3:10, where believers are "becoming like Christ in his death."

a mark of the Christian life. Believers are to live lives of "obedience, which leads to righteousness" (6:16; cf. 15:18). Paul points to the obedience of Jesus Christ as the basis of our justification: "By the one man's obedience the many will be made righteous" (5:19). We are to obey God with the epoch-making obedience of Jesus in mind.

A second term that connects imitation of Christ to Christian living is Paul's use of the standard Jewish metaphor for godly conduct—namely, *walking*. In two instances, the recommended manner of conduct is informed by the example of Christ. The pattern of dying to sin and rising to a new way of living, "walk[ing] in newness of life," is based on the template of Christ's life story (6:4). In the other instance, we are to "walk properly" by "putt[ing] on the Lord Jesus Christ" (13:13–14). Clothing yourself with Christ is to be inspired and informed by the exemplary conduct of Jesus Christ. In Romans, Paul depicts "the Christian life lived out under the authority of Jesus as Lord and in conformity to him as an inevitable corollary of the gospel."[8]

Conclusion

Romans describes three pillars that together form a firm foundation on which Paul's teaching about the Christian life is built. Dying and rising in union with Christ give us our identity and the template of our life stories. Being led by the Spirit gives us what we need in our fleshly existence to put sin to death. And the exemplary life and death of Jesus our Lord supply content and direction for walking in love and obedience. The fruit of living in accordance with our identity in Christ, being led by the Spirit, and being conformed to the image of God's Son lead "to holiness and in the end eternal life" (6:22 my translation). These gospel truths strengthen us to end the reign of sin in our lives.

8 James D. G. Dunn, *The Theology of Paul the Apostle* (Grand Rapids, MI: Eerdmans, 1998), 650.

12

The Gospel and Life Together

Let love be genuine.

ROMANS 12:9

THE LOVE OF GOD IS CENTRAL to the gospel in Romans. Paul writes to "all those in Rome who are loved by God" (1:7)—a unique description of the recipients of Paul's letters. He presents God's love (5:5, 8; 8:39) and Christ's love (8:35, 37) as the motives for the plan of salvation. Unsurprisingly, then, Paul's vision of the Christian life in Romans can be summed up in one word: love. We love God (8:28) and others because God first loved us. Paul himself is a model of love for fellow Christians, regularly addressing them—both as a group (12:19) and as individual men and women (16:5, 8, 9, 12)—as "beloved" (*agapētos*). And the Christians in Rome are repeatedly urged to loving conduct (12:9; 13:8 [2x], 9, 10 [2x]), a love that the Spirit inspires (15:30). They are to walk in love (14:15) and to love their enemies (12:17–21).[1] In a brief span, Paul repeats the call to love four times, using four different words: "Let love [*agape*] be genuine. . . . Love one another with brotherly [and sisterly] affection [*tē philadelphia eis allēlous philostorgoi*]. . . . Show hospitality [*philoxenia*—literally, "love for strangers"]" (12:9–10, 13). And Paul

1 Although the word "love" doesn't appear in 12:17–21, Paul's instructions about behavior toward one's enemies are an application of 12:9: "Let love be genuine."

urges believers to "owe no one anything, except to love each other" (13:8), explaining that "love . . . is the fulfillment of the law" (13:10 CSB).

The most explicit practical teaching in the letter appears in Romans 12–16, where the central injunction is a call to express genuine love (12:9). However, we must not read this portion of the letter in isolation, for as we saw in chapter 11 above in connection with dying and rising with Christ, Paul's instructions about how to walk and please God are firmly rooted in gospel truths. It is a serious mistake to treat Paul's ethics as unrelated to his doctrine since one flows out of the other. Yet again, a cumulative reading of Romans is required for a full appreciation of Paul's theology.

Paul's moral teaching in Romans is the direct outworking of his gospel. Its presentation, both in terms of the topics Paul chooses and their expression, is particularly suited to the Roman Christians. As Michael Bird contends, Paul's teaching in Romans 12–15 is "a vision of how the Roman house churches can indigenize the Pauline evangelical mission in Rome as it relates to relationships within and outside the community, in the seat of empire, surrounded on all sides by disbelieving Jews and suspicious pagans."[2]

In considering Paul's teaching on the Christian life, we will focus on particular passages in Romans 12–16 with frequent reference to Romans 1–11. In this chapter, we concentrate on Paul's teaching on loving one another in Romans 12:1–16 and 14:1–15:7. In chapter 13, we will look at his instructions about loving your enemies (12:14, 17–21), submission to human government (13:1–7), and the implicit call to promote the gospel and support missionary endeavors (15:8–16:16). The focus on eschatology in chapter 14 includes 13:11–14, a passage about the need for godly conduct in light of the imminent return of Christ.

Responding to the Mercies of God

> I appeal to you therefore, brothers [and sisters], by the mercies of God, to present your bodies as a living sacrifice, holy and acceptable to God, which is your spiritual worship. Do not be conformed to

2 Michael F. Bird, "Echoes and Allusions to the Jewish Scriptures in Paul's Ethical Discourse in Rom 12:9–21," in *Scripture, Texts, and Tracings in Romans*, ed. Linda L. Belleville and A. Andrew Das (London: Lexington, 2021), 180.

> this world, but be transformed by the renewal of your mind, that by testing you may discern what is the will of God, what is good and acceptable and perfect. (12:1–2)

This passage marks a clear turning point. An inferential conjunction, "therefore" (*oun*), connects a reference to the mercies of God in the previous context (a key concept in Rom. 9–11; see 9:15, 16, 18, 23; 11:30, 31, 32) to an appeal for conduct in keeping with the gospel of God's mercy. Indeed, it is striking how many thematic connections there are between 12:1–21 and 13:8–14, on the one hand, and the portrait of pagan sin in 1:18–32, on the other. Paul's vision of the Christian life is a reversal of the moral degradation of the sin of idolatry, a turning from sin to serve the true and living God. Side by side, the passages are an illustration of the true repentance and transformation that the gospel brings (see table 12.1).

Table 12.1 Comparison of Romans 1:18–32 and Romans 12:1–21; 13:8–14

Romans 1:18–32	**Romans 12:1–21; 13:8–14**
The wrath of God (1:18)	The mercies of God (12:1)
Bodies dishonored (1:24)	Bodies presented as holy (12:1)
Idolatrous worship (1:23, 25)	Spiritual worship (12:1)
Futile thinking (1:20); a debased mind (1:28)	A renewed mind (12:2)
The righteous decree of God ignored (1:32)	The will of God discerned and approved (12:2)
Insolent and boastful (1:30)	Not thinking too highly of yourself (12:3); not haughty but associating with the lowly (12:16)
Haters of God (1:30)	Haters of evil (12:9)
Heartless (1:31)	Genuine love (12:9)
Dishonouring their bodies (1:24)	Showing honor (12:10)
Inventors of evil (1:30); filled with evil (1:29)	Overcomers of evil with good (12:21)
Committing shameless acts (1:27)	Walking decently (13:13)
Lustful hearts given to impurity (1:24)	Resisting the desires of the flesh (13:14)

Paul opens his exhortation in 12:1 by addressing the Roman Christians as brothers and sisters (*adelphoi*), a designation he repeats eleven more times in Romans 12–16. Far from merely perfunctory, as Trevor Burke notes, "the frequency with which the early Christian movement in general, and the apostle Paul in particular, employed this expression [brothers and sisters] is unprecedented."[3] Its usage probably derives from the precedent of the same language in the Old Testament for Israel as the people of God and from the teaching of Jesus that his followers are a new family (cf. Matt. 12:46–50). In Romans, "[t]he members of the communities were *adelphoi* [brothers and sisters] because Jesus is the firstborn Son (Rom 8:29)."[4] The language of brothers and sisters is also related to the experience of having God as our Father (cf. Rom. 8:12–15). In Romans, sibling language connotes love and intimacy among fellow believers (12:10 CSB: "Love one another deeply as brothers and sisters"), is used to call for the avoidance of conflict (14:10, 13, 15, 21; 16:17), and is the grounds for the exercise of mutual care and support (15:14, 30). According to Paul, brothers and sisters in Christ must respond to the mercies of God by living the good life, thinking rightly about themselves, and loving one another sincerely.

The Good Life

The question of what constitutes a good life is one of perennial interest. In the ancient world, the concept of the good life was discussed at length by the likes of Socrates, Plato, Aristotle, and their followers. They debated whether a good life consists primarily of things like health, wealth, and beauty or whether virtue and character are more important. In our day, positive psychology has generated the happiness movement, which seeks to discover how to live a life filled with purpose, wellbeing, and joy. Romans uses the language of "the good" (*agathos*) in several places for something of high moral value or merit, something useful

3 Trevor Burke, *Family Matters: A Socio-Historical Study of Kinship Metaphors in 1 Thessalonians*, LNTS (London: T&T Clark, 2003), 174.

4 Paul Trebilco, *Self-Designations and Group Identity in the New Testament* (Cambridge: Cambridge University Press, 2003), 66.

or beneficial. God works things together for our good (8:28). We are to "hold fast to what is good" (12:9), "overcome evil with good" (12:21), "do what is good" (13:3), please our neighbors for their good (15:2), and "be wise as to what is good" (16:19). In 12:1–2 we are to prove that God's will for our lives is good. What these two verses teach about the good life can be summarized in seven points.

First, the good life requires urging. Paul's opening appeal in 12:1 (cf. 15:30) uses the word *parakaleō*, which can be translated "appeal to, urge, exhort, encourage."[5] This is no surprise, given the deep plight of humanity under sin, our life in the flesh, and the powers ranged against us (see chapters 2 and 3 above). The good life is not a set-and-forget project. Specific actions concerning pride, the use of gifts, love, patience, generous giving, love of enemies, and so on is urged throughout the rest of Romans 12. In similar terms Paul implores the Roman Christians to fight against sin and present themselves to God: "Use your whole body as an instrument to do what is right for the glory of God" (6:13 NLT).

Second, the good life is lived together with others. Paul calls for the presentation of "your" bodies to God (12:1)—the pronoun is plural—which he then explains in terms of body life (using their gifts for the benefit of others) and group action. Most of the instructions in 12:1–21 are only possible when undertaken corporately. For example, we are to contribute to, bless, rejoice with, and live in harmony with others (12:13–16).

Third, the good life is a response to "the mercies of God" in the gospel (12:1). As we saw in chapter 11, God's gracious provision of our union with Christ and life in the Spirit is the foundation on which good can triumph over sin and evil in our lives.

Fourth, the good life requires total dedication of our lives as an act of worship. As James Dunn notes, the Christian notion of sacrifice in 12:1 has been transposed in two ways: "from cultic ritual to everyday life, from a previous epoch characterized by daily offering of animals

5 "Παρακαλέω," in BDAG 765.

to one characterized by a whole-person commitment lived out in daily existence."[6]

Fifth, the good life is countercultural. Believers are not to "copy the behavior and customs of this world" (Rom. 12:2 NLT) or "conform to the evil desires you had when you lived in ignorance" (1 Pet. 1:14 NIV).[7] Culture is an invisible and largely unnoticed force that influences our thinking and ways of living, many of which are inimical to God's will and harmful to ourselves and others. Only lives marked by total dedication, testing, and discernment—that is, mind renewal—can hope to sift out and counter its damaging impacts.

Sixth, the good life requires thinking differently. Our behavior is transformed by the renewal of our minds (12:2). Paul made the same point earlier: "Those who live according to the flesh set their minds on the things of the flesh, but those who live according to the Spirit set their minds on the things of the Spirit" (Rom. 8:5). Paul recognizes that we behave in a certain way because we believe certain things. His gospel in Romans gives believers the "powers of discernment [that train them] by constant practice to distinguish good from evil" (Heb. 5:14).

Seventh, the good life is God's will for our lives, which is "good, pleasing and perfect" (12:2 NIV)—that is, good for us, pleasing to him, and perfect ("meeting the highest standards"[8]) in God's sight. According to Rebecca McLaughlin, psychological studies confirm that the basics of Christian living—loving relationships, helping others, forgiving others, being thankful, being generous, and living for something bigger than yourself—make you happier, healthier, live longer, and be less likely to suffer depression.[9] Living this way also pleases God, as Paul makes clear in 14:18 using the same adjective as in 12:2: "Anyone who serves Christ in this way [i.e., living to build up others in 14:17] is *pleasing*

6 James D. G. Dunn, *Romans 9–16*, WBC (Dallas: Word, 1988), 710.

7 The verb "to conform" occurs in these two verses in the New Testament (Rom. 12:2; 1 Pet. 1:14).

8 "Τέλειος," in BDAG 995.

9 Rebecca McLaughlin, *Confronting Christianity: 12 Hard Questions for the World's Largest Religion* (Wheaton, IL: Crossway, 2019), 17–31.

to God" (NIV). Such living is "perfect" in the sense that it expresses God's own nature and his intentions for human life.

How to Think about Yourself

As noted in chapter 3, for Paul there is no individual outside of community and no community without individuals at the heart of its ongoing life. Hence in 12:3–8, Paul offers instruction for how to think about yourself as an individual in community. He warns against having too inflated an opinion of yourself and recommends one informed by "sober judgment" (12:3). We should acknowledge that each of us has a measure of faith as a gift from God and has gifts from God for the service of others. Instead of belonging to ourselves, we belong to each other in the body of Christ. Paul sees living for and contributing to the lives of others—a highly countercultural idea in a society obsessed with looking only inward to discover your authentic self—as the path to true self-knowledge.[10]

In Romans 12:6–8 Paul lists seven gifts to illustrate his point that each of us has a part to play in the healthy functioning of the body of Christ. Different lists appear in other letters (see 1 Cor. 12:7–10, 28; Eph. 4:11), with only prophecy and teaching overlapping with the list in Romans 12, suggesting that the gifts named here are representative and not a precise or exhaustive inventory. The way to exercise each of the seven gifts is reinforced with a distinctive phrase, the overall force of which is to underscore the need for Christians to use their gifts with gusto. Those with the gifts of serving, teaching, and encouragement are to devote themselves to service, teaching, and encouragement. The other four gifts have different qualifiers. Those who prophesy require faith, those who give must do so generously, those who lead must do so diligently, and the merciful must stay cheerful. These guidelines offer theological and emotionally intelligent insight into the respective gifts and the ideal conditions for their proper exercise.[11]

10 See Brian S. Rosner, *How to Find Yourself: Why Looking Inward Is Not the Answer* (Wheaton, IL: Crossway, 2022).

11 E.g., the merciful are perhaps prone to melancholy due to the nature of their helping others in difficult situations.

All You Need Is Love

In Romans 12:9–16, Paul offers instructions as to how to love one another sincerely, without pretending (*anupokritos* in 12:9). Indeed, "Let love be sincere" (12:9 my translation) can be thought of as the heading for all of the exhortations to follow. Romans 12:9–13 contains imperatival participles that can be translated as fleshing out the manner in which genuine love is to be expressed: by abhorring evil, holding fast to the good, being devoted to one another, honoring one another, being zealous and fervent in spirit, serving the Lord, rejoicing in hope, being patient in tribulation and constant in prayer, contributing to the needs of the saints, and showing hospitality. Then he commands showing love to one's enemies (12:14, 17–21). Paul's work of collecting money to bring "aid to the saints" (15:25) in Jerusalem is a practical expression of sincere love (see 15:25–28).

What to Do When Christians Differ

In Romans 14:1–15:7 Paul teaches how Christians ought to behave toward fellow believers when they hold different views on matters of legitimate dispute. While some things for Paul are of "first importance" (cf. 1 Cor. 15:1–7), others are of a secondary nature. With respect to the latter, believers are to welcome one another (14:1; 15:7).

The disputable matters that Paul treats concern two topics in particular—namely, the restriction of diet (14:2, 21) and observing certain days in preference to others (14:5). In the scenario Paul paints, "the weak" in the church (probably mainly Christians from a Jewish background) kept Jewish kosher laws and observed the Sabbath; "the strong" (mainly Gentile Christians) did not. Paul actually counts himself among the strong (15:1) and is convinced that the Christian believer may "eat anything" (14:2). His position is made clear earlier in Romans where he asserts that believers in Christ are not under the law (6:14–15; 7:1–6). Still, on such matters, each individual is to act in accordance with his or her own convictions (14:5–6). As Paul states, "The faith that you have, keep between yourself and God" (14:22). In effect, Paul allows for the expression of Jewish cultural tradition, where one lives under the law's direction but not its dominion.[12] Whether Paul is responding to a report of such arguments among the Roman Christians or simply giving teaching to forearm them based on his experience of Jewish and Gentile converts adjusting to not being under the law is difficult to tell with certainty.

Christians ought not despise or judge one another on disputable matters: "The one who eats everything [the strong] must not despise [*exoutheneō*[13]] the one who does not [the weak], and the one who does not eat everything [the weak] must not judge [*krinō*] the one who does [the strong], for God has accepted that person" (Rom. 14:3 my translation; cf. 14:10).

Paul is concerned that the weak, the more conservative group, not "judge" the strong, the less conservative group. The weak believed that certain days were sacred and special (14:5–6) and that some foods were forbidden according to God's law. For them to disregard such laws would be an act of disobedience to God. When they saw other Christians acting in defiance of such laws, they were tempted to judge (i.e., condemn) them as disobedient to God. Paul is just as concerned about the behavior of the strong. The strong are the less conservative group, taking a less strict line on the application of Jewish food and Sabbath laws. Paul tells them not to despise the weak, the more conservative group. From their point of view, the strong would easily have regarded the weak as not taking the freedom of the gospel seriously enough and of merely being wedded to their cultural background.

Paul asks incredulously of both parties, "Who are you to pass judgment on the servant of another? It is before his own master that he stands or falls" (14:4). He insists that ultimately each Christian lives

12 See Brian S. Rosner, *Paul and the Law: Keeping the Commandments of God*, NSBT 31 (Downers Grove, IL: IVP Academic, 2013), 45–82.

13 The verb in question, *exoutheneō*, is translated variously (Rom. 14:3, 10) as "despise" (NRSV; ESV), "treat with contempt" (NIV), and "look down on" (CSB). It is used elsewhere in the New Testament of the self-righteous "looking down" on everyone else (Luke 18:9 CSB) and of Jesus being "ridiculed" by Herod and the soldiers at his trial (Luke 23:11 NIV). Clearly, it is not behavior of which the early Christians approved.

as one directly accountable to God. The point is underscored with the use of the phrase "to the Lord / to God" (both datives of advantage in the Greek): "Whoever regards one day as special does so *to the Lord*" (14:6 NIV). When we judge or despise another believer on a disputable matter we are effectively usurping their true ownership and allegiance. In one sense, what they think about such things is none of our business! God will hold them to account.

Paul makes clear that Christian leaders are permitted to teach clearly on matters of dispute. In the midst of a unit in which he insists that believers must have their own convictions before God, Paul declares his own stance quite openly: "I know and am persuaded in the Lord Jesus that nothing is unclean in itself" (14:14a). Then he avers, "But it is unclean for anyone who thinks it unclean" (14:14b). Paul is not forcing his own views on the weak. In the HCSB, Romans 14:14 is in parentheses, suggesting that it is an aside in Paul's main argument. We may teach a position on a disputable matter but, according to Paul's example, not insistently. We should teach "in parentheses," so to speak.

In 15:1–7 Paul moves from a focus on individual responsibility toward God to a communal focus. In Paul's view, at least in the case of the strong, some flexibility may be needed. Speaking to the strong, and including himself, Paul reasons that we may need to vary our practice in certain settings: We are not just "to please ourselves" (15:1). Rather, we "should please our neighbors for their good, to build them up" (15:2 NIV). In doing so, we act in imitation of Christ, who "did not please himself" (15:3). The big command in the passage appears in 14:19: "Let us pursue what makes for peace and for mutual upbuilding." The implication is clear: To squabble will lead to strife and demolish the church.

Paul reinforces his instructions on not squabbling over disputable matters by pointing to three things that will be seriously impaired if he is not heeded: (1) the health and happiness of the church, (2) the progress of the gospel, and (3) the glory of God. In order to give both sides some perspective, Paul plays down the significance of the food laws and tells the Christians in Rome what is truly important in the kingdom of God: "For the kingdom of God is not food and drink but righteousness and peace and joy in the Holy Spirit" (14:17 my translation). Paul believes that squabbling over secondary matters puts at risk the health and happiness of the church.

For Paul's mission to succeed, he needs the Roman Christians—both Jews and Gentiles—to welcome one another and not squabble so that with one mind and voice they might glorify God (15:6). Paul's ultimate purpose in dealing with the quarrels in the churches in Rome is not to smooth things over; rather, it is that "the Gentiles might glorify God" (15:9; cf. 15:6, 7). The apostle makes clear that this will be achieved by sorting out certain ethical problems: "Welcome one another . . . for the glory of God" (15:7). Four Old Testament quotations in 15:9–12 reiterate the goal of Gentiles praising God along "with his people" (15:10). United churches are a precondition for the effective proclamation of the gospel to the glory of God.

With respect to disputable matters, in Romans 14–15, Paul stresses the need for personal convictions, flexibility, not judging or despising those who disagree, and the goal of peace and edification. As it turns out, the theological foundations of his teaching on disputable matters are remarkably profound. Doctrine matters, especially when it comes to disputable matters. Paul appeals to the lordship of Christ, the imitation of Christ, justification by faith, and the work of the Spirit in the kingdom of God. The whole passage explains what it means to walk in love (14:15) when disagreements arise in church life.

Conclusion

"Let love be genuine" (Rom. 12:9) is a good summary of Paul's vision of gospel living in the body of Christ. Indeed, if not for the famous encomium to love in 1 Corinthians 13, Romans 12 could be labelled Paul's quintessential love chapter.[14] As it turns out, the two passages cover much the same ground in describing love in action. Both present love as opposing evil (Rom. 12:9; 1 Cor. 13:6), rejoicing in hope (Rom. 12:12; 1 Cor. 13:7, 8–13), being patient (Rom. 12:12; 1 Cor. 13:4), being

14 In the NET Bible, Rom. 12:9–21 is entitled "Conduct in Love."

kind and generous to others (Rom. 12:13; 1 Cor. 13:3, 4), not being arrogant (Rom. 12:16; 1 Cor. 13:4), and not retaliating or keeping a record of wrongs (Rom. 12:19–21; 1 Cor. 13:5). Giving honor to others (Rom. 12:10) is also implicitly commended in 1 Corinthians as an expression of love (1 Cor. 12:23, 24, 26). And when Paul comes in Romans 14 to the topic of disagreements among Christians, his instructions may be summed up as "walking in love" (Rom. 14:15).

13

Gospel Living in the World

Live peaceably with all.

ROMANS 12:18

PAUL'S VISION OF THE CHRISTIAN LIFE is not one of loving only other believers and withdrawing from the world (cf. 1 Cor. 5:10). His gospel has profound implications for how we relate to people and entities outside the church. In this chapter, we look at Paul's instructions about gospel living in the world. Paul covers three topics in Romans 12–16: He calls on the Roman Christians to love their enemies (12:14, 17–21), submit to human government (13:1–7), and promote the gospel (15:8–16:16). In line with the practice of reading Romans cumulatively, I will make frequent reference to other passages in the letter to get the full picture of gospel living in the world.

Love Your Enemies

Romans 12:14 introduces the subject of loving your enemies: "Bless those who persecute you; bless and do not curse them." However, in 12:15–16 Paul gives further instruction on love between brothers and sisters in Christ, before providing motivation for loving your enemies in 12:17–21.[1]

1 12:17–21 is marked off as a subunit by the repetition of two occurrences of "evil" in 12:17 and 12:21.

While some argue that 12:15–16 also concerns behavior toward outsiders, the use of the reflexive pronoun, *allelōn*, points to community harmony being in view: "Live in harmony with *one another*" (12:16). This command is repeated in 15:5. Indeed, Paul's "one another" teaching in Romans (and elsewhere) is about love in the community: Believers are members of one another (12:5) who ought to love one another deeply (12:10), honor one another (12:10), build up one another (15:2), welcome one another (15:7), instruct one another (15:14), greet one another affectionately (16:16), and not judge one another (14:13). (We looked at 12:15–16 in chapter 11.)

In 12:17–21 Paul instructs the Christians in Rome on how to respond to those who wish to do them harm. Quoting two Old Testament passages (Deut. 32:15 in Rom. 12:19; Prov. 25:21–22 in Rom. 12:20), Paul urges believers to take the difficult path of loving their enemies in the hope of turning them into friends with four striking antitheses:

- "Bless those who persecute you; bless and do not curse them" (12:14).
- "Repay no one evil for evil, but give thought to do what is honorable in the sight of all" (12:17).
- "Never avenge yourselves, but leave it to the wrath of God" (12:19).
- "Do not be overcome by evil, but overcome evil with good" (12:21).

Once again, Paul's moral teaching flows from his theology. We are to love our enemies in imitation of God. At the heart of the gospel is the fact that "God shows his love for us in that while we were still sinners, Christ died for us. . . . While we were [God's] enemies we were reconciled to God by the death of his Son" (5:8, 10). Believers love their enemies because God loved us when we were his enemies.

Paul urges not just non-retaliation but doing good to those who intend to do you evil. Clearly, he recognizes how difficult this is when he admits that living at peace with everyone is sometimes not possible and will depend in part on the response of one's enemies (12:18). To help the Roman Christians follow his difficult advice, Paul exhorts them to think differently about the common human desire to take revenge. Instead of retaliating, believers should trust in the God of perfect justice to put things right in his own time: "Leave it to the wrath of God" (12:19). This is not a contradiction to do good to our enemies or to forgive them. Rather, it paves the way for overcoming evil with good and kind responses by giving believers somewhere to park their grievances and longing for justice.

Paul closes his advice with a pithy and poignant saying: "Do not be overcome by evil, but overcome evil with good" (Rom. 12:21).[2] Peter Stuhlmacher is right that this exhortation "is based on the conduct and example of Jesus,"[3] most clearly expressed at his crucifixion at the hands of his enemies (see Luke 23:34). Romans 12:14 and 12:21 also echo the teaching of Jesus, who told his disciples, "Love your enemies, do good to those who hate you, bless those who curse you" (Luke 6:27–28; cf. Matt. 5:44).

Submit to Government

Romans 13:1–7 is sometimes regarded as a jarring deviation from Paul's treatment of relating to outsiders in a way that is in keeping with the gospel. Whereas the priority of love in relationships (with both believers and nonbelievers) dominates 12:1–21 and 13:8–10, Paul instructs the Roman Christians to submit to government in 13:1–7: "Let every person be subject to the governing authorities" (13:1). Some regard the passage as a later interpolation. More concerning, 13:1–7 has a checkered history of interpretation. In commanding submission to government, "over the centuries it is has often been used to support the divine right of kings, blind nationalism, and unquestioned loyalty to rulers—even tyrants."[4] Where does 13:1–7 fit in Paul's teaching on

2 Cf. B. M. Newman and E. A. Nida. *A Handbook on Paul's Letter to the Romans* (New York: United Bible Societies, 1973), 243: "This verse is best taken as a summary statement of what Paul has said in verse 17–20."

3 Peter Stuhlmacher, *Paul's Letter to the Romans: A Commentary*, trans. Scott J. Hafemann (Edinburgh: T&T Clark, 1994), 198.

4 Michael J. Gorman, *Romans: A Theological and Pastoral Commentary* (Grand Rapids, MI: Eerdmans, 2022), 252.

gospel living in the world? Does Paul see the Roman authorities as all-powerful rulers enabled by God to exercise their power in any way they deem fit? What does the passage actually teach about the Christian view of government?

Appeal is often made to two ways of reading the passage that attempt to soften its seemingly absolute call to compliance with Roman government, "in all its brutal strength."[5] First, it has been pointed out that Paul was writing in the late AD 50s, "well before the persecution under Nero, which began in 64."[6] While this may explain, in part, Paul's teaching and manner of expression, the passage is nonetheless a general message about governing authorities being "instituted by God" (13:1)—labeling them as servants of God (13:4)—and it mirrors the view of Old Testament wisdom literature. Second, some argue that "the primary purpose of the passage is narrow: a call for believers in Rome to pay their taxes (13:6–7) rather than resist paying them (13:2, 4)."[7] However, paying taxes in 13:6–7 is an illustration of being in subjection to government mentioned in 13:5. Furthermore, government wielding "the sword" (13:4) to punish "bad" (*kakos*, 13:3) behavior is too broad to be applied only to failure to pay a tax. Paul's comments on government cannot be limited to the task of tax collecting.

A faithful reading of 13:1–7 requires that it be read in its literary context with the rest of Romans in mind, noting carefully what it says and does not say. The text is linked to the preceding context with several shared terms. Both passages commend conduct that is "good" (*agathos*, 12:2, 9, 21; 13:3, 4) and not "evil" (*ponēros*, 12:9; *kakos*, 12:17, 21; 13:3, 4), command showing honor (*timē*, 12:10; 13:7), and address the notion of taking vengeance (12:17, 19; 13:4).

The big interpretive issue is whether "Paul's words [in 13:1–7] invite uncritical devotion to, or worship of, any political person or entity."[8]

5 Helen Paynter, *Blessed Are the Peacemakers: A Biblical Theology of Human Violence*, BTFL (Grand Rapids, MI: Zondervan Academic, 2024), 211.

6 Paynter, *Blessed Are the Peacemakers*, 212.

7 Gorman, *Romans*, 254–55.

8 Gorman, *Romans*, 256.

Many commentators rightly insist that 13:1–7 is only part of Paul's (and the New Testament's) view of government, citing the counterbalancing negative view of the Roman Empire in Revelation 13 and the example of Peter and the apostles, who "obey God rather than men" (Acts 5:29) when the two are at odds with each other. The theme of God's comprehensive and exhaustive judgment of all evil in Romans 1–3 suggests that the authorities themselves in 13:1–7 are not beyond critique. That God is opposed to all forms of evil is an established presupposition in Romans. Immediately before 13:1–7, Paul emboldens believers to "overcome evil with good" (12:21).

Furthermore, the emphasis on the lordship of Christ in Romans (and elsewhere in Paul's letters) is rightly taken as having an anti-imperial edge. Michael Bird points out that some of Paul's gospel terminology has both Old Testament background and Greco-Roman resonances (in propaganda relating to the Caesar), including "lord," "gospel," and "savior."[9] "Jesus is Lord" (10:9) would have been heard as insisting, or at least implying, that Caesar is not! As Gorman notes, "Simply to confess Jesus as Lord and royal Messiah has political implications."[10]

Significantly, Paul says that "submission" is owed to government and not "obedience" in all circumstances, suggesting "a more generalized posture."[11] To submit is to recognize that someone has authority over you. Paul reserves the language of obedience in Romans to what we owe to God alone. The passage says that government, as "God's servant" (13:4), is due respect and honor (13:7) but—conspicuously, in view of the emperor cult in Rome—not worship. "Paul's perspective certainly does not make any Roman rulers—not even the Emperors—divine."[12]

9 Michael F. Bird, *A Bird's-Eye View of Paul: The Man, His Mission and His Message* (Leicester, UK: Inter-Varisity Press, 2008), 86–88. See also Christoph Heilig, *The Apostle Paul and the Empire: Paul's Implicit and Explicit Criticism of Rome* (Grand Rapids, MI: Eerdmans, 2022).

10 Gorman, *Romans*, 252.

11 Paynter, *Blessed Are the Peacemakers*, 211.

12 Gorman, *Romans*, 255.

More positively, the partial perspective that 13:1–7 offers is that "God gives government as a gift to humanity to bring welfare, safety, order and justice to human communities."[13] As history has taught us repeatedly, "Almost any form of government is better than anarchy."[14] We are to submit to government and thank God for it. At the same time, we learn in 13:1–7 that government's authority is derivative, not definitive. Rulers too, as ministers of God, will face God's judgment and may even deserve subversive resistance when they are a terror to good conduct and do evil.

Paul's call to submit to government as God's servant in 13:1–7 is an application of his commands to love genuinely (12:9) and live peaceably (12:18). It answers two questions: What are the conditions in society under which love and peace can thrive? And how can Christians support such arrangements? It is not a blanket endorsement of all governments. The critique of bad government, while not explicit, is implied in the language Paul uses in the passage and in the broader context of the teaching of Romans on God's righteous judgment and the lordship of Christ.

Promote the Gospel

The last main section of the letter, 15:8–16:27, covers Paul's missionary calling, travel plans, and final greetings. Although the passage does not focus on a particular aspect of the gospel, we have seen the relevance of the section for the letter's purpose (see chapter 1 on 16:25), the inclusive nature of the gospel (see chapter 3 on the diverse range of personal greetings in 16:1–16), the scriptural roots of the gospel (see chapter 5 on 16:25–26), and the expression of genuine love among believers (see chap. 12). Furthermore, the section contains important information about believers' final victory in Christ (see chapter 14 on 16:20). It is also of interest, as we shall see, for the topic of gospel living in the world.

13 N. T. Wright and Michael F. Bird, *Jesus and the Powers: Christian Political Witness in an Age of Totalitarian Terror and Dysfunctional Democracies* (Grand Rapids, MI: Zondervan, 2024), 152.

14 Wright and Bird, *Jesus and the Powers*, 152.

Paul does not call on the Roman Christians to preach the gospel. Indeed, his letters use the *euangel-* terminology ("preach the gospel" and "evangelist") exclusively for authorized heralds of the good news, following the messenger traditions of LXX Isaiah 40:9; 52:7; 61:1.[15] Romans 10:15, quoting Isaiah 52:7, makes this clear: "And how are they to preach unless they are sent? As it is written, 'How beautiful are the feet of those who preach the good news [*euangelizomenōn ta agatha*]!'"

However, it is not that believers who are not authorized to preach the gospel have no part to play in the spread of the gospel. As John Dickson puts it, "Although *proclamation* of the gospel, on the part of believers generally, is never implied in Paul's letters, *promotion* of the gospel certainly is."[16] Paul encourages the Roman Christians, as his partners in the gospel (cf. Phil. 1:5), to promote it in three ways. This teaching in Romans is more implied than explicit but can be discerned from the space Paul devotes to certain subjects and his manner of expression.

First, Paul encourages the Roman believers to promote gospel work by his honoring of gospel workers in their midst and by urging their support of those in gospel ministry.[17] The extensive greetings in Romans 16 not only reveal "Paul's collaborative style of ministry, including ministry with women,"[18] but also include fascinating descriptions of many of those engaged in Christian service (see table 13.1). Some of those designated Paul's fellow workers were likely authorized heralds with experience of proclaiming the gospel. Paul's lengthy description of his own missionary work and ongoing agenda (15:14–21) and his request that the Roman Christians support his mission to Spain (15:24) are further evidence that he expects them to support gospel work, including the provision of financial assistance.[19]

15 Cf. John P. Dickson, *Mission-Commitment in Ancient Judaism and in the Pauline Communities*, WUNT 2/159 (Tübingen: Mohr Siebeck, 2003), 311.

16 Dickson, *Mission-Commitment*, 311 (emphasis in original).

17 "How are they to preach unless they are sent?" (Rom. 10:15).

18 Gorman, *Romans*, 292.

19 The verb translated "to help on a journey" (*propempō*) is also used in this technical sense in 1 Cor. 16:6, 11; 2 Cor. 1:16.

Table 13.1 Christian Workers/Service in Romans 16

Name	Designation/role
Phoebe (16:1–2)	A servant or deaconess of the church at Cenchreae; patron of many and of Paul
Prisca and Aquila (16:3–5)	Paul's fellow workers in Christ Jesus; house church hosts
Mary (16:6)	Worked hard for the Roman Christians
Andronicus and Junia (16:7)	Paul's fellow prisoners; well known to/among the apostles
Urbanus (16:9)	Paul's fellow worker in Christ
Apelles (16:10)	Approved in Christ
Tryphaena and Tryphosa (16:12)	Workers in the Lord
Persis (16:12)	Worked hard in the Lord
Mother of Rufus (16:13)	Acted as a mother to Paul

Second, Paul encourages the Roman Christians by his own example to pray for unbelievers. "Prayer for the salvation of others was, by the apostle's own enthusiastic confession, part of Paul's private piety."[20] In 10:1 he interrupts his indictment of the Jews and offers a heartfelt entreaty: "Brothers [and sisters], my heart's desire and prayer to God for them is that they may be saved." Paul undoubtedly also prayed for the salvation of Gentiles and expected all believers to do so.

Third, Paul expects all Christians to adorn the gospel by living lives worthy of the gospel. The reputation of the church, the gospel, and God are unavoidably, if sometimes regrettably, intertwined. Such connections can be seen by analogy with Israel in 2:17–24, where Paul lists the hypocrisy and law breaking of the Jews and concludes with a quotation from Isaiah that "the name of God is blasphemed among the Gentiles because of you" (Rom. 2:24, quoting Isa. 52:5). Paul and Isaiah believe that the bad behavior of God's people reflects badly on God. If the Roman Christians behave badly, the progress of the gospel will be impeded.

20 Dickson, *Mission-Commitment*, 215.

The reverse is also true: Good behavior of the people of God propels the gospel of God. That behavior toward outsiders can also act as an ethical apologetic is suggested in 12:17 and 12:20–21, where loving your enemies may even lead to their repentance.

Conclusion

Living in a manner worthy of the gospel requires genuine love not only toward fellow believers but all people. Christians are to love their enemies, live peaceably with all, and support the spread of the gospel.

14

The Gospel and the End of All Things

The day is at hand.

ROMANS 13:12

"THE END OF ALL THINGS" (1 Pet. 4:7) is not the main focus of any one passage or section in Romans. Indeed, Romans is more often cited in connection with other themes. Other Pauline epistles, such as 1–2 Thessalonians, are better known for their teaching about eschatology. However, a closer look reveals that Romans has much to say about the final phase of Paul's gospel of salvation. Hope, for example, is a big theme, with the verb "to hope" (*elpizō*) and the noun "hope" (*elpis*) appearing frequently across the letter.[1] Paul argues that hope is a benefit of the gospel (Romans 5, 8; see chapter 8 above), tells the Roman Christians to "rejoice in hope" (12:12), contends that the Old Testament was written to give us hope (15:4), and declares that his mission is to enable Gentiles to hope in the Messiah (15:12). Indeed, Paul desires that "the God of hope" will use his letter to fill believers with joy and peace and to abound in hope (15:13).

Every section of Romans contributes to the subject of eschatology. Paul uses a number of themes and images to bring home the message that "salvation is nearer to us now than when we first believed" (13:11).

1 The words occur more often than in any other letter of Paul—seventeen times out of a total of fifty-five.

Far from marginal and dispensable parts of Paul's gospel, these subjects explored below are intrinsic to the story of salvation and draw on material from across the letter.

Judgment and Condemnation

In chapter 2 we considered the universal human condition of being under the penalty of sin. In this section I briefly summarize the teaching of Romans on judgment and condemnation.

Romans teaches that "the day of wrath when God's righteous judgment will be revealed" (2:5; cf. 12:19) is inescapable for the unrepentant (2:3). If all human beings are unrighteous (3:5, 9–18), God's judgment is marked by perfect righteousness (3:5). The law is no use in escaping God's wrath (4:15). Only Jesus Christ's death and risen life can save us from the wrath of God (5:9). In sum, the unrepentant will suffer "condemnation" (3:8; 5:16, 18), a verdict that does not apply to those who are in Christ Jesus (8:1).[2]

However, even though God's kindness, forbearance, and patience will lead some to repentance (Rom. 2:4), all must face judgment and give an account of their lives: "We will all stand before the judgment seat of God" (Rom. 14:10). The purpose of this judgment is "so that each one may receive what is due for what he has done while in the body, whether good or evil" (2 Cor. 5:10). In the context of Romans 14, Paul uses the final appraisal of the lives of believers to dissuade them from prematurely judging each other on disputable matters; each is accountable directly to God for his or her behavior, as a slave is accountable to a master (Rom. 14:10, 12). The judgment of believers should be distinguished from the judgment of those who do not obey the gospel (Rom. 10:16). The former does not result in their condemnation (Rom. 8:1), for even if the work of a believer is burned up, "he himself will be saved" (1 Cor. 3:15).

Death and Life

In Romans as in 1 Corinthians 15, "The resurrection of Jesus Christ stands as the central motif in Paul's eschatology insofar as it inaugu-

2 The words used for "condemnation" in these verses include *krima* (3:8) and *katakrima* (5:16, 18; 8:1).

rates the age to come and provides the basis for future hope."[3] Indeed, Jesus's resurrection plays a key role in the argument of Romans in five ways, culminating in the promise of the resurrection and eternal life of believers:[4]

1. The resurrection of Jesus is the basis for Paul's apostleship (1:4–6). "The risen and powerful messianic Lord has bestowed the grace of apostleship on Paul with the purpose of advancing his universal dominion over all the nations through the preaching of the gospel."[5]
2. The resurrection of Jesus is the confirmation of God's righteous verdict upon believers (4:17–25). Jesus was "raised for our justification" (4:25). Just as God vindicates Jesus by raising him from the dead, publicly declaring him righteous, so too those who are in union with Christ by faith are declared righteous in him.
3. Faith in the resurrection of Jesus is part of a believing response to the gospel (10:7–9). "If you confess with your mouth that Jesus is Lord and believe in your heart that God raised him from the dead, you will be saved" (10:9).
4. The resurrection of Jesus is the basis for the inclusion of the Gentiles in the people of God (15:8–12). Quoting Isaiah 11:10, Paul describes Jesus as "he who rises to rule the Gentiles" (Rom. 15:12 my translation).
5. The resurrection of believers is tied to the resurrection of Jesus (6:4–10, 7:4, 8:11; 14:9–11). "To this end Christ died and lived again, that he might be Lord both of the dead and of the living" (14:9). A big part of the argument of 5:12–8:39 is that "just as believers have been granted the verdict of righteousness-vindication that was proclaimed in the resurrection of Jesus so too believers

3 Larry J. Kreitzer, "Resurrection," *DPL* 806.

4 Cf. the helpful overview in Peter M. Head, "Jesus' Resurrection in Pauline Thought: A Study in the Epistle to the Romans," in *Proclaiming the Resurrection*, ed. Peter M. Head (Carlisle, UK: Paternoster, 1998), 58–80.

5 Head, "Jesus' Resurrection in Pauline Thought," 63.

will be rescued from death and granted a part in the resurrection life of Jesus."[6] In Romans 6 we die and rise with Christ so that "we too might walk in newness of life" (6:4), both now and forever.

Day and Night, Darkness and Light

In Romans 13:11–14, Paul urges believers to behave in ways that are in keeping with their new identity as those who belong to the age to come: "Because we belong to the day, we must live decent lives for all to see" (13:13 NLT). In making his appeal in 13:11–14, Paul uses four interrelated images: waking from sleep, putting on the amor of light, walking in the daylight, and putting on the Lord Jesus Christ.[7] Consistent with the primary metaphor of darkness and light, four of the shameful deeds that are unsuitable to daytime people typically take place in the nighttime: orgies, drunkenness, sexual immorality, and sensuality. The next two vices, "quarrelling and jealousy" (13:13) are concerns that Paul addresses in the following section of the letter (14:1–15:7).

Paul's appeal sits under the rubric of knowing what time it is (13:11). In fact, much of Paul's teaching, not least in Romans, is framed around two-time schemas: the once/now of pre-Christian and Christian existence[8] and the already / not yet of living in the kingdom of God in a dark world in anticipation of the full and bright manifestation of that kingdom. Paul speaks of "the present time" (3:26) in which God has saved us through the redemption in Christ and of Christ dying for the ungodly "at the right time" (5:6).[9] The "great and terrible day" (Mal. 4:5 CSB) of Christ's return—darkness for some, light for others (cf. Amos 5:18)—is a theme with a long backstory in the Old Testament. Paul describes it in Romans as "the day of wrath" (2:5) and "the day when . . . God judges the secrets of men by Christ Jesus" (2:16). He uses familiar and memorable imagery as another reason for believers

6 Head, "Jesus' Resurrection in Pauline Thought," 70.

7 The language of "putting on" evokes the image of getting dressed.

8 E.g., Rom. 7:5–6 (NIV): "We were in the realm of the flesh. . . . But now . . . we serve in the new way of the Spirit."

9 Elsewhere he urges that now is "a favorable time . . . a day of salvation" (2 Cor. 6:2).

not to let sin reign in our lives: "The night is far gone; the day is at hand" (13:12). We are to remember that we belong to the day and behave accordingly.

Metaphors in Romans

In studying the theology of Romans, it is common for interpreters to prioritize literal and direct discourse and treat figurative language as mere illustration—"icing on the cake" that adds little to Paul's teaching. But this is mistaken. As a good communicator Paul routinely relates his message in concrete and relatable familiarity using figures of speech. The metaphors in Romans are a good example.

Metaphors actually communicate more meaning than propositional language rather than less. Rightly understood, they inform and also move the hearer. Metaphors have an affective impact in addition to carrying cognitive meaning. By appealing to something that is concrete and known, like all figurative language, a good metaphor is easily recalled and sticks in the mind. The keys to the interpretation of a metaphor are its literary context and cultural milieu—often informed by prior usage in the Old Testament.[a]

As already noted in chapter 4, Paul uses a range of images for salvation in Romans, drawing on legal (justification), slave market (redemption), relational (reconciliation), and temple (mercy seat) settings. In fact, the entire letter is punctuated, or adorned, with metaphorical language. The extended metaphor or parable of the olive tree in 11:11–24 is a prime example of the elaborate use of agricultural imagery (see chapter 10 for its interpretation). Table 14.1 offers a summary of metaphorical language in Romans from thirteen realms of human experience.

Table 14.1 Metaphors in Romans[b]

Realm of imagery	Usage in Romans
Political	Covenant, gospel, and kingdom language
Military	Enemies (5:10); war (7:23); sword (8:35; 13:4); weapons (6:13); conquerors (8:37); armor (13:12)
Legal	Righteousness, judge, condemnation, etc.
Cultic	Heaven, worship, sacrifice, priestly service, etc.
Kinship	Adoption, childbirth, servants/slaves, siblings, offspring, etc.
Transport	Roads, paths, and ways (3:2, 16–17); footsteps and following (4:12); walking (6:4; 8:4; 13:13; 14:15); stumbling and obstacles (9:32; 11:9, 11; 14:13, 20; 16:17)
Work	Work (20x); potter (9:20–21).
Finance	Wages (4:4, 8; 6:23), debt (4:8; 8:12–13; 15:27), riches (2:4; 9:23; 10:12; 11:12, 33)
Construction	Building stone (9:33); foundation (15:20); building others up (14:19; 15:1–2, 20)
The body	Body, flesh, mouth, tongue, lips, ears, hearing, eyes, heart, neck, hands, legs, feet, toes, backs
Geology	Sand and sea (9:27); stones and rocks (9:32–33)
Fauna	Asps (3:13), sheep (8:36)
Agriculture and food	Fruit and harvest (1:13; 6:21–22; 7:4–5; 15:28; 16:5); firstfruits (8:23; 11:16); lumps of dough (11:16); roots and branches (11:16; 15:12)

a On Paul's metaphors see Brian S. Rosner, *Greed as Idolatry: The Origin and Meaning of a Pauline Metaphor* (Grand Rapids, MI: Eerdmans, 2007); Brian S. Rosner, *Known by God: A Biblical Theology of Personal Identity*, BTFL (Grand Rapids, MI: Zondervan, 2017), chap. 9.

b This list builds on Mark J. Keown, *Romans and the Mission of God* (Eugene, OR: Wipf and Stock, 2021), 59–62; David J. Williams, *Paul's Metaphors: Their Context and Character* (Peabody, MA: Hendrickson, 1999).

Creation and New Creation

In Romans 8:19–23 Paul reveals that the hope of the gospel extends beyond human salvation to the renewal of all of creation. Graham Cole explains, "Paul personifies creation under the figure of a pregnant woman about to give birth. Creation's destiny is intertwined with that of God's children. The Christian hope is not for the individual alone but has cosmic implications."[10]

That the gospel hope encompasses all creation is not an isolated afterthought in Romans. The promise to Abraham is for his offspring to be "heir of the world" (4:13), and God graciously gives believers "all things" (8:32). The theme of new creation is one that has deep roots in the Old Testament (cf. Isa. 65–66).

Divine Glory

Romans opens with a reference to the tragic exchanging of "the glory [*doxa*] of the immortal God" for the worship of mortal creatures (1:23) and closes with an exuberant ascription of "glory forevermore" to "the only wise God" (16:27; cf. 11:36). God is rich in glory (9:23), and even human sin can magnify God's glory (3:5). The theme of glory is another subplot of Romans, moving from the tragic loss of God's glory to eschatological glory for God's people and God's creation.[11]

Idolatry is an offense against the God of glory (1:23). Human beings, without distinction (3:22), "lack [*hustereō*] the glory of God" (3:23 my translation). This determination reflects the Jewish tradition that God's glory was originally reflected in the face of Adam—because he was made in the image of God—and was lost at the fall. Thus, believers, as a result of being justified by faith, "rejoice in hope of [experiencing and being restored to] the glory of God" (5:2).

Romans 8 fills out the picture of the glorious future of God's people. As H. Jacob observes, "believers' union with Christ is fundamental to Paul's

10 Graham A. Cole, *The God Who Became Human: A Biblical Theology of Incarnation*, NSBT (Downers Grove, IL: IVP Academic, 2013), 147.

11 See Haley Goranson Jacob, *Conformed to the Image of His Son: Reconsidering Paul's Theology of Glory in Romans* (Downers Grove, IL: IVP Academic, 2018).

understanding of their [future] glory. . . . The glory the children of God will have is due to their participation in the glory of the firstborn Son."[12]

> If children, then heirs—heirs of God and fellow heirs with Christ, provided we suffer with him in order that we may also be glorified with him.
>
> For I consider that the sufferings of this present time are not worth comparing with the glory that is to be revealed to us . . . that the creation itself will be set free from its bondage to corruption and obtain the freedom of the glory of the children of God. (8:17–18, 21)

In this light, the glorification of those who love God in 8:28–30 should be seen in part as their participation in the Son's inheritance of ruling over the earth in the new creation (cf. 1 Cor. 6:2: "The world is to be judged by you").[13]

The Crushing of Satan

> The God of peace will soon crush Satan under your feet. (Rom. 16:20)

> I will put enmity between you [the serpent] and the woman,
> and between your offspring and her offspring;
> he shall bruise your head,
> and you shall bruise his heel. (Gen. 3:15)

In the letter closing of Romans, immediately before the final greetings (16:21–23) and doxology (16:25–27), Paul offers a striking benediction in 16:20 that alludes to Genesis 3:15.[14] It contains several unexpected elements: the God "of peace" undertakes the violent action against Satan, under "the feet" of the Roman Christians, and this will happen "soon"! In eleven short words (fourteen in Greek), Paul recalls major gospel themes in Romans, including the work of Christ, union with

12 Jacob, *Conformed to the Image of His Son*, 369.

13 The case is put in full by Jacob, *Conformed to the Image of His Son*.

14 Cf. chapter 3 for Paul's use of Gen. 1–3 in Rom. 5–8.

Christ, suffering in the Christian life, the use of the Old Testament, and God's final victory over evil. Thus, the promise is a fitting way to round off our survey of the teaching of Romans on the gospel and the end of all things.

Paul's promise of the victory of believers over evil picks up and draws together ideas from two specific texts in Romans 12 and 13. First, in 12:17–21 Paul points to God's decisive eschatological action against evil: "Leave room for God's wrath" (12:19 CSB). He also holds out the prospect of believers having a part in overcoming evil themselves: "Do not be overcome by evil, but overcome evil with good" (12:21). In this way, the promise in 16:20 of God defeating evil in connection with the activity of believers brings to mind the earlier text in Romans and is a fitting further encouragement for believers to do good in the present.[15]

Second, a similar link can be seen between 16:20 and 13:11–14. In 13:11–14 Paul calls on Christians to behave well in the light of the coming eschaton, doing battle with the evils of self-indulgence and social strife. Then, in 16:20 he repeats that the final victory will occur "soon" and the end of all evil is in sight. When the Roman Christians heard Paul's sure promise of this future victory in the letter closing they would have taken it as further encouragement to live in ways (mentioned in 13:11–14) that are in keeping with that coming day.

Yet 16:20 is not entirely good news, even if it includes believers in God's ultimate triumph over Satan and evil. For, in God's crushing of Satan under the feet of believers lurks the suspicion that the battle will not be without some cost. Indeed, Genesis 3:15 sets the tone for the verse as one of mutual hostility between the serpent and Eve's offspring:

> I will put enmity between you and the woman,
> and between your offspring and her offspring.

15 The reference to "evil" in 12:21 picks up the occurrences of the same word in 12:17: "Repay no one evil for evil." Given the widespread association of Satan with evil across the New Testament and the use of "the evil one" as a moniker for Satan (e.g., Matt. 5:37; 6:13; John 17:15; Eph. 6:16; 2 Thess. 3:3; 1 John 2:13, 14; 3:12; 5:18, 19), it is significant that in Rom. 12:21 believers triumph over evil.

When read in the light of Genesis 3:15, where the serpent bruises the heel of Adam's seed, Romans 16:20 can be seen to include the sobering implication that the victory of believers over such a formidable adversary will involve some personal distress. However, Paul has prepared the Roman Christians well for dealing with this reality through his profound teaching about the suffering of believers in union with Christ. Extensive treatments of the beneficial purpose of such suffering occurs in 5:3–5 and 8:12–39 (see chapter 8 above), where suffering is seen to be "the divinely orchestrated means by which God strengthens their faithful endurance and hope by pouring out his own love and Spirit to sustain or deliver them in their distress."[16]

If 16:20 reminds the Christians in Rome of the travails of their lives as those in union with Christ in waiting for God's imminent victory, the recollection of Romans 8 would comfort them that their suffering is the pathway to sharing in Christ's glory: "Who shall separate us from the love of Christ? Shall tribulation, or distress, or persecution, or famine, or nakedness, or danger, or sword?" (8:35)

"The God of peace will soon crush Satan under your feet" (16:20). These words strike notes of joy and hope, recalling key texts in Romans that summarize several major themes in the letter. Paul reminds the Roman Christians of their deliverance by God from the power of sin as those in union with Christ, urging them to understand the present time by overcoming evil and doing good. He also reminds them to be comforted in their suffering—all in light of the reassurance that the night is almost over and the day will soon be here.

16 S. J. Hafemann, "Suffering," in *DPL* 920.

Epilogue

Strengthened by the Gospel

To him who is able to strengthen you according to my gospel.

ROMANS 16:25

THE APOSTLE PAUL had a broad and varied job description. He worked as a tentmaker, letter writer, community founder, collection curator, networker, team leader, traveler, sage, and so on. Perhaps his two most important roles, both related to his commission from Jesus Christ, were missionary and pastor. Paul's prodigious activity in these two callings can be summed up in two verbs: preach and strengthen. As a missionary he was sent to "preach the gospel" (*euangelizō*) to those who did not know Christ (Rom. 15:20; cf. 1 Cor. 1:17), and as a pastor he sought "to strengthen" (*stērizō*) with the gospel those who had already come to faith in Christ. Those in Rome to whom he wrote belonged to Christ already (Rom. 1:6–7); therefore, his purpose in writing Romans was to strengthen them with his gospel (1:11, 15; 16:25; see above introduction on the purpose of Romans).

That Paul sought to strengthen believers with the gospel is clear from the other four uses of the verb *stērizō* in his letters (1 Thess. 3:2, 13; 2 Thess. 2:17; 3:3) and from Luke's description of Paul's visits to churches in Acts (14:22; 15:32, 41; 18:23) where Luke regularly employs the related verb *epistērizō*. In these texts, God is the one who strengthens, encourages, and comforts believers with the gospel, thereby equipping them for every good work and to live holy lives, protected from the evil one. This is a remarkably good summary of the intent of the theology of Romans.

The Power of God in the Gospel

As it turns out, power and strength are key concepts in Paul's exposition of the gospel in Romans.[1] The gospel is about the powerful Son of God (1:4) and God's power to save those who believe the good news (1:16). Although human beings refuse to acknowledge God's power (1:20), Abraham is a model believer in being "fully convinced that God had the power to do what he had promised" (4:21 my translation) when he "grew strong in his faith" (4:20). The Lord has the power to make believers, both Jews and Gentiles, stand before him justified and forgiven (14:4). God's power liberates us from the law, the flesh, sin, death, and Satan (Rom. 6–8; 16:25). This gospel spreads "by the power of the Spirit of God" (15:19). There are no powers capable of separating believers from God's love (8:35–39). Even if many Israelites have rejected his Messiah, "God has the power to graft them in again" (11:23). Just as the gospel displays God's power, God's work in the history of salvation makes his power known (9:17, 22).[2]

Paul also teaches that believers receive a kind of gospel power to exercise their gifts, build others up, love their enemies, and so on. And "by the power of the Spirit" they "abound in hope" (15:13). It is important to note that, when exercised in social contexts, divine power is "not power 'over' others but power 'on behalf' of others."[3] Believers overcome evil not by force but by doing good (12:21). The power of God is most clearly seen in God's sending his Son "in the likeness of sinful flesh" as a sin offering (8:3). The cross shows that power is not to be exercised selfishly or oppressively but in love and the service of others.

1 See Beverly Roberts Gaventa, "Places of Power in Paul's Letter to the Romans," *Int* 76, no. 4 (2022): 293–302.

2 All of the "power" references in this paragraph use the noun *dunamis* ("power"), the verb *dunateō* ("to be able"), or the adjective *dunatos* ("able, capable, powerful").

3 Gaventa, "Places of Power," 301.

The Gospel of God

What, then, is Paul's gospel in Romans that he believed would strengthen believers? The gospel of God is a public announcement about Jesus Christ, and its main function is to save. Romans unpacks that gospel and shows how it strengthens those who believe the good news.

All human beings, as descendants of Adam, both Jews and Gentiles, exist under the condemnation and power of sin and live under the reign of death. We need deliverance from God's righteous anger and from an oppressive enslavement to sin. The gospel is the work of God; we are saved by God's grace, mercy, kindness, and love. God the Father planned our salvation, God the Son achieved it, and God the Spirit implements it by giving us new life now and forever.

To be saved is to be justified, forgiven, counted as righteous, redeemed, set free, adopted into God's family, reconciled, united to Christ, made holy, given eternal life, and granted honor and glory. The present benefits of the gospel are no less remarkable: peace with God, access to God's grace, a sure hope, the joy of beneficial suffering, the gift of the Holy Spirit, the assurance of God's love, and (best of all) knowing and being known by God.

The one who saves us is Jesus, the long-awaited Messiah, the Lord, the Son of God, the deliverer, the stone of stumbling, the last Adam, the servant to the circumcised, and God over all. Jesus died as our substitute, as the mercy seat and sin offering, as our representative, and as an example of sacrificial love—to reveal God's righteousness and love. Jesus rose from the dead to reveal his true identity, to confirm our justification, to inaugurate the new creation, to conquer evil, to commence his rule in the kingdom of God, and to give us new life. And Jesus ascended to make intercession for us, and he will return in glory. At every step the gospel accords with and is the fulfilment of the Law and the Prophets.

We are saved by the amazing grace of God, which is superabundant, antecedent, incongruous, and efficacious. And we respond in believing trust—that is, repenting of our sins, being baptized, confessing Jesus as

Lord, calling on his name, giving glory to God for his promises, putting our hope in the Messiah, and receiving God's gracious gift with thanksgiving. Israel's disappointing failure to respond to the gospel is neither full nor final; there is hope for Israel based on God's sovereign, faithful, and merciful character.

The life-giving Holy Spirit of God and Christ makes believers children of God and fellow heirs with Christ; supplies righteousness, peace, and joy to the people of God; assures them of God's love; and imparts holiness to them. The gospel enables believers to end the reign of sin in their mortal bodies through living by the Spirit, union with Christ in his death and resurrection, and being conformed to the image of Christ.

Responding to the gospel mercies of God, believers are to live lives marked by genuine love and affection for each other, abhorring evil, holding fast to the good, being devoted to one another, honoring one another, being zealous and fervent in spirit, serving the Lord, rejoicing in hope, being patient in tribulation and constant in prayer, contributing to the needs of the saints, and showing hospitality. They are to walk in love, even amid sharp disagreements. They are to live peaceably with all, loving their enemies, submitting to government, supporting the spread of the gospel, and living as those who belong to the fast-approaching day of salvation.

Made Strong by the Gospel

The three ugliest vice lists in Paul are in Romans 1:29–31; Galatians 5:19–21; and 2 Timothy 3:2–4. Romans 1:29–31 describes the lifestyle of those who reject God (see chapter 2 above), and Galatians 5:19–21 lists the works of the flesh. The list in 2 Timothy 3:2–4 is perhaps the most disturbing because it describes people who claim to be Christians: They are "lovers of self, lovers of money, proud, arrogant, abusive, disobedient to their parents, ungrateful, unholy, heartless, unappeasable, slanderous, without self-control, brutal, not loving good, treacherous, reckless, swollen with conceit, lovers of pleasure rather than lovers of God." Such people have "the appearance of godliness" but reject the "power" (*dunamis*) of God that could make them godly (2 Tim. 3:5). In

Romans 16:25, Paul reveals the source of such power: God strengthens Christians through the gospel.

God not only justifies, redeems, and reconciles us through the gospel but also gives us the strength we need for the Christian life through the gospel. Only the gospel gives us a clear-sighted view of our fleshly existence, our moral incapacity and weakness, and the means of dealing with our guilt and shame. Only the gospel sets us free from sin's power when we present ourselves to God as those who have been brought from death to life in union with Christ. Only the gospel enables us to cast off the works of darkness by putting on the Lord Jesus Christ. Only the gospel gives us a mind set on the Spirit which is life and peace. Only the gospel punctures our pride, helping us to recognize that God has given us gifts for the service of others. Only the gospel calls us to walk in love found in Christ's unforgettable example of sacrificial love in dying for us. Only the gospel places us in a transformative, countercultural community of people of all ages and backgrounds with the same life story of dying and rising with Christ. Only the gospel of God's reconciling love enables us to love our enemies, knowing that the God of all justice will one day put the world to right. Only the gospel supports our weak and faltering prayers with the intercession of both Christ and the Spirit. Only the gospel gives meaning to our suffering and the comfort of the sure hope of the glory of God. Only the gospel gives us a secure identity as God's beloved children. Only the gospel gives us a story worth living. Only the gospel gives lasting meaning to our lives—namely, a small part to play in God's grand story of redeeming love.

In the letters that follow Romans in the New Testament, Paul strengthens believers in diverse settings and contexts by applying the truths of the gospel to their lives. Paul exhorts the Christians in Colossae, "As you received Christ Jesus the Lord, so walk in him, rooted and built up in him and established in the faith, just as you were taught, abounding in thanksgiving" (Col. 2:6–7). John Piper, preaching on Romans 16:25, puts it well:

> The heart of the gospel is that Jesus Christ, the righteous one, died for our sins and rose again, eternally triumphant over all his enemies,

> so that there is now no condemnation, but everlasting joy, for those who trust him. You never, never, never outgrow your need for this gospel. You don't begin the Christian life with this and then leave it behind and get stronger with something else. God strengthens us with the gospel to the day we die.[4]

In Romans, we meet Paul the missionary and pastor. He writes to the Roman Christians of his plans to visit them on his way to Spain to preach the gospel where Christ has not already been named. To get them on his side and to strengthen and encourage them in their faith, he imparts to them the spiritual gift of preaching the gospel to them. That same gospel has the power in our day to fill us with all joy and peace in believing and cause us by the power of the Holy Spirit to abound in hope.

4 John Piper, "God Strengthens Us by the Gospel" (sermon, Bethlehem Baptist Church, Minneapolis, MN, November 26, 2006), https://www.desiringgod.org/.

Recommended Resources

Commentaries

Bird, Michael F. *Romans*. SGBC. Grand Rapids, MI: Zondervan Academic, 2016.

Gorman, Michael J. *Romans: A Theological and Pastoral Commentary*. Grand Rapids, MI: Eerdmans, 2022.

Moo, Douglas J. *The Epistle to the Romans*. 2nd ed. NICNT. Grand Rapids, MI: Eerdmans, 2018.

Peterson, David G. *Commentary on Romans*. BTCP. Nashville: Holman Reference, 2017.

Schreiner, Thomas R. *Romans*. 2nd ed. BECNT. Grand Rapids, MI: Baker Academic, 2018.

Stuhlmacher, Peter. *Paul's Letter to the Romans: A Commentary*. Edinburgh: T&T Clark, 1994.

Monographs

Barclay, John M. G. *Paul and the Gift*. Grand Rapids, MI: Eerdmans, 2015.

Barclay, John M. G. *Paul and the Power of Grace*. Grand Rapids, MI: Eerdmans, 2020.

Blazosky, Bryan. *The Law's Universal Condemning and Enslaving Power: Reading Paul, the Old Testament, and Second Temple Jewish Literature*. University Park, PA: Eisenbrauns, 2019.

Gupta, Nijay K., and John K. Goodrich, eds. *The Beginning of Paul's Gospel: Theological Explorations in Romans 1–4*. Eugene, OR: Cascade, 2023.

Jervis, L. Ann. *The Purpose of Romans: A Comparative Letter Structure Investigation*. JSNTSup 55. Sheffield: JSOT Press, 1991.

Keener, Craig S. *The Mind of the Spirit: Paul's Approach to Transformed Thinking*. Grand Rapids, MI: Baker Academic, 2016.

Keown, Mark J. *Romans and the Mission of God*. Eugene, OR: Wipf and Stock, 2021.

Mininger, Marcus A. *Uncovering the Theme of Revelation in Romans 1:16–3:26*. WUNT 445. Tübingen: Mohr Siebeck, 2017.

Moo, Douglas, J. *A Theology of Paul and His Letters: The Gift of the New Realm in Christ*. BTNT. Grand Rapids, MI: Zondervan Academic, 2021.

Moo, Douglas J., Eckhard Schnabel, Frank Thielman, and Thomas R. Schreiner, eds. *Paul's Letter to the Romans: Theological Essays*. Peabody, MA: Hendrickson Academic, 2023.

Rosner, Brian S. *Paul and the Law: Keeping the Commandments of God*. NSBT. Downers Grove, IL: IVP Academic, 2013.

Schreiner, Thomas R. *Paul, Apostle of God's Glory in Christ: A Pauline Theology*. 2nd ed. Downers Grove, IL: IVP Academic, 2020.

Timmins, Will N. *Romans 7 and Christian Identity: A Study of the 'I' in Its Literary Context*. SNTSMS. Cambridge: Cambridge University Press, 2017.

Weima, Jeffrey A. D. *Paul the Ancient Letter Writer: An Introduction to Epistolary Analysis*. Grand Rapids, MI: Baker Academic, 2016.

Windsor, Lionel J. *Paul and the Vocation of Israel: How Paul's Jewish Identity Informs His Apostolic Ministry, with Special Reference to Romans*. BZNW 205. Berlin: de Gruyter, 2014.

General Index

Scripture Index

OLD TESTAMENT PSEUDEPIGRAPHA

New Testament Theology

The Beginning of the Gospel
MARK

From the Manger to the Throne
LUKE

The Mission of the Triune God
ACTS

Strengthened by the Gospel
ROMANS

Ministry in the New Realm
2 CORINTHIANS

Christ Crucified
GALATIANS

United to Christ, Walking in the Spirit
EPHESIANS

Sharing Christ in Joy and Sorrow
PHILIPPIANS

Hidden with Christ in God
COLOSSIANS AND PHILEMON

To Walk and to Please God
1 AND 2 THESSALONIANS

The Appearing of God Our Savior
1 AND 2 TIMOTHY AND TITUS

Perfect Priest for Weary Pilgrims
HEBREWS

Living Faith
JAMES

The God Who Judges and Saves
2 PETER AND JUDE

The Joy of Hearing
REVELATION

Edited by Thomas R. Schreiner and Brian S. Rosner, this series presents clear, scholarly overviews of the main theological themes of each book of the New Testament, examining what they reveal about God and his relation to the world in the context of the overarching biblical narrative.